Note to parents

by working through this learn to write
workbook
your child will:

- Create a fondation for future learning

-Gain exposure to the alphabet

-Develop motor skills

want free goodies email us
at itsmareze@gmail.com
title the email learn to write
workbook

Questions and customer
service email us at
itsmareze@gmail.com

Tracing Letters

Practice writing the alphabet by tracing the letters below.

Aa Bb Cc Dd

Ee Ff Gg Hh

Ii Jj Kk Ll

Mm Nn Oo Pp

Qq Rr Ss Tt

Uu Vv Ww Xx

Yy Zz

DIRECTIONS: PRACTICE WRITING EACH LETTER IN THE SPACE PROVIDED.

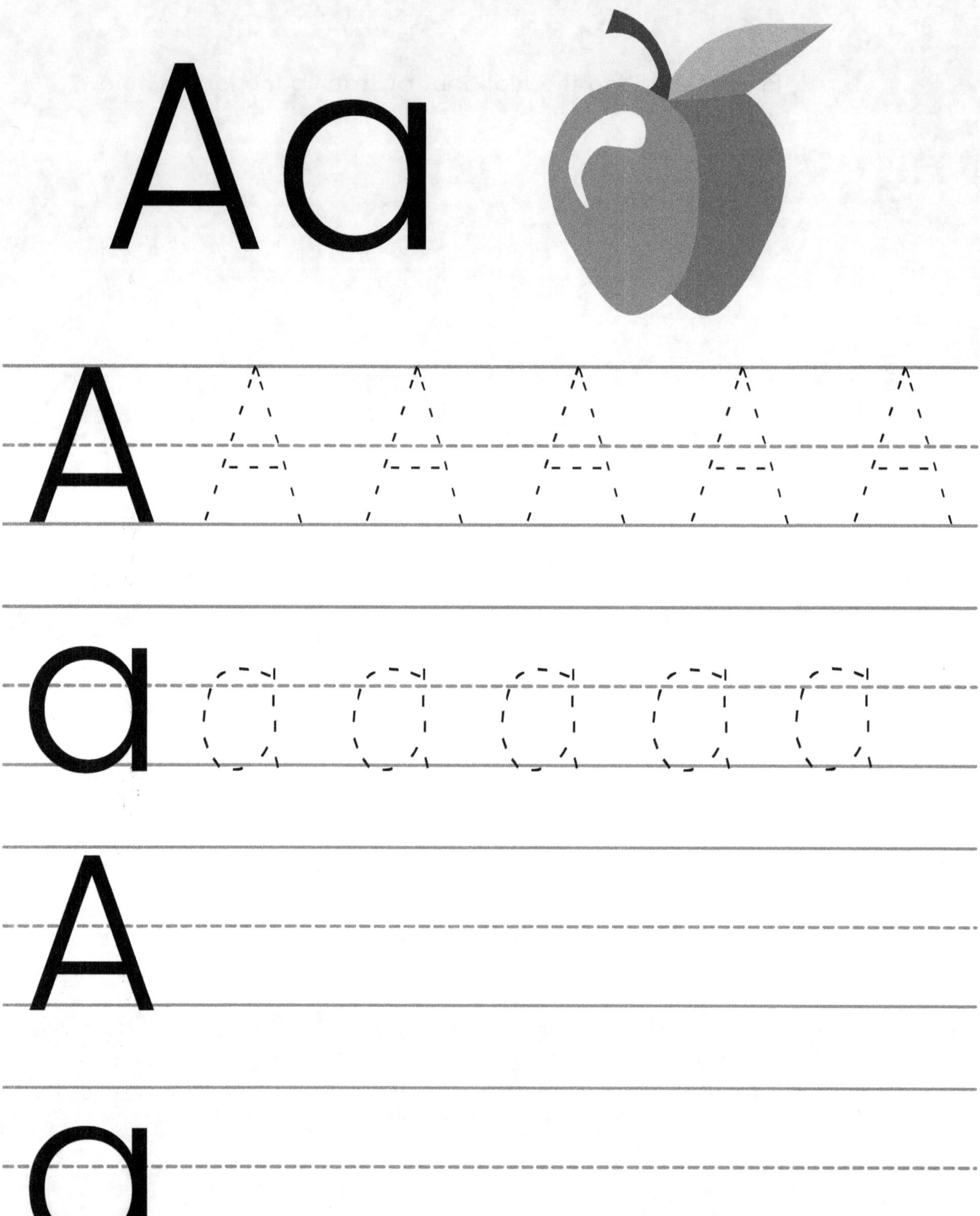

DIRECTIONS: TRACE THE WORDS THAT BEGIN WITH THE LETTER A

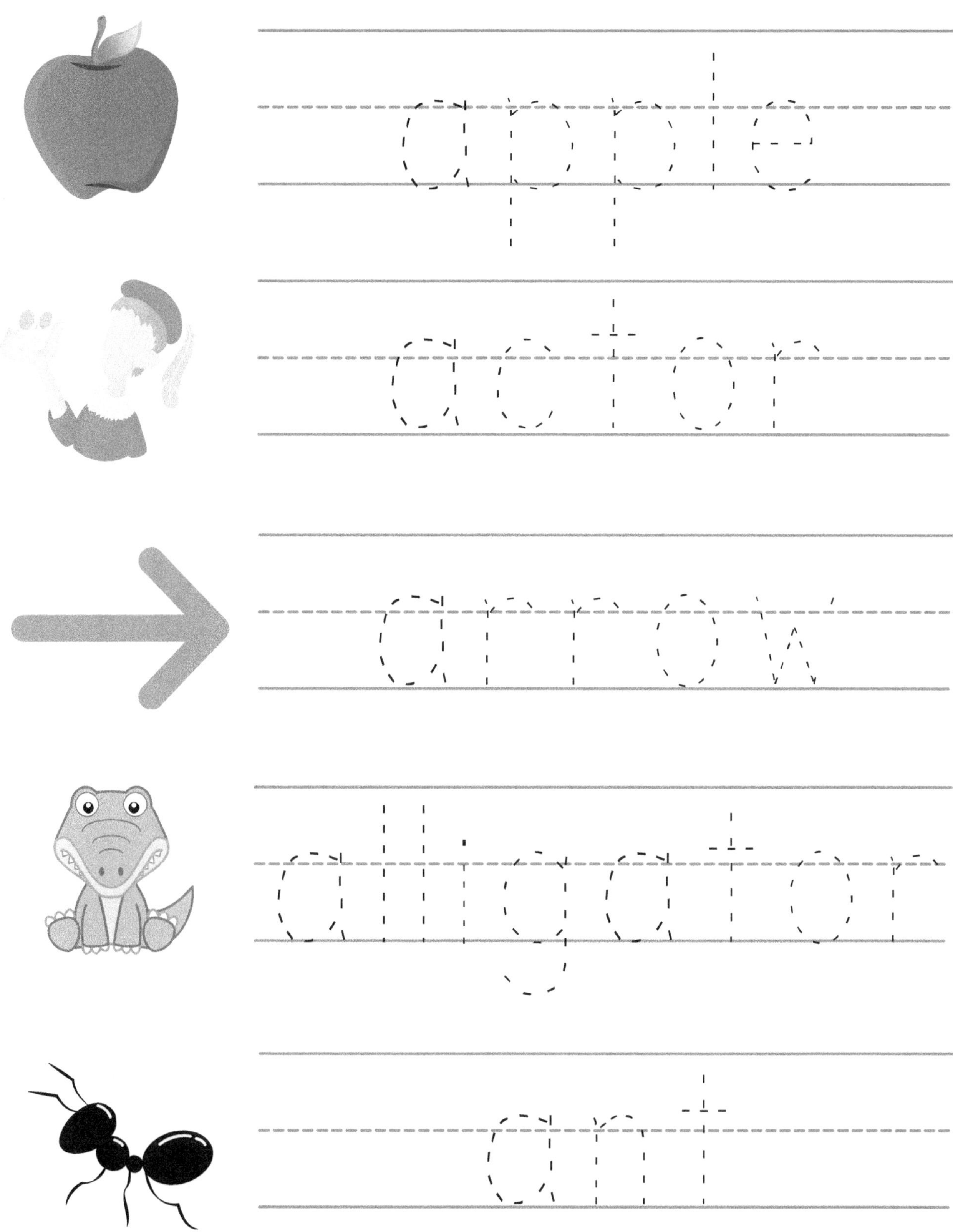

FIND THE LETTERS.

DIRECTIONS: TRACE THE LETTERS. THEN COLOR THE
CIRCLES THAT HAVE THE LETTER YOU TRACED.

is for
Apple

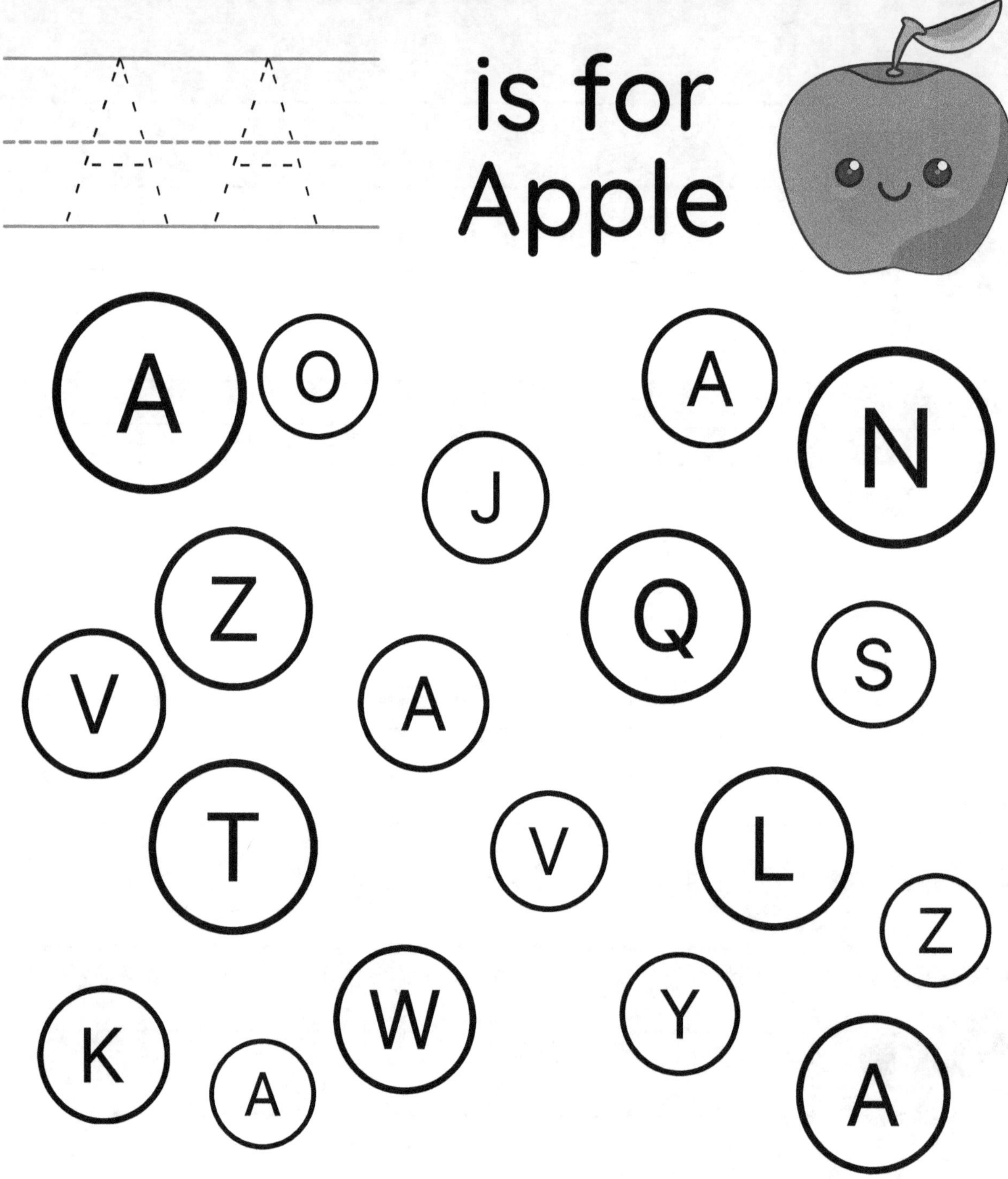

Bb

B B B B B B B B B B

b b b b b b b b b

B

b

DIRECTIONS: TRACE THE WORDS THAT BEGIN WITH THE LETTER B

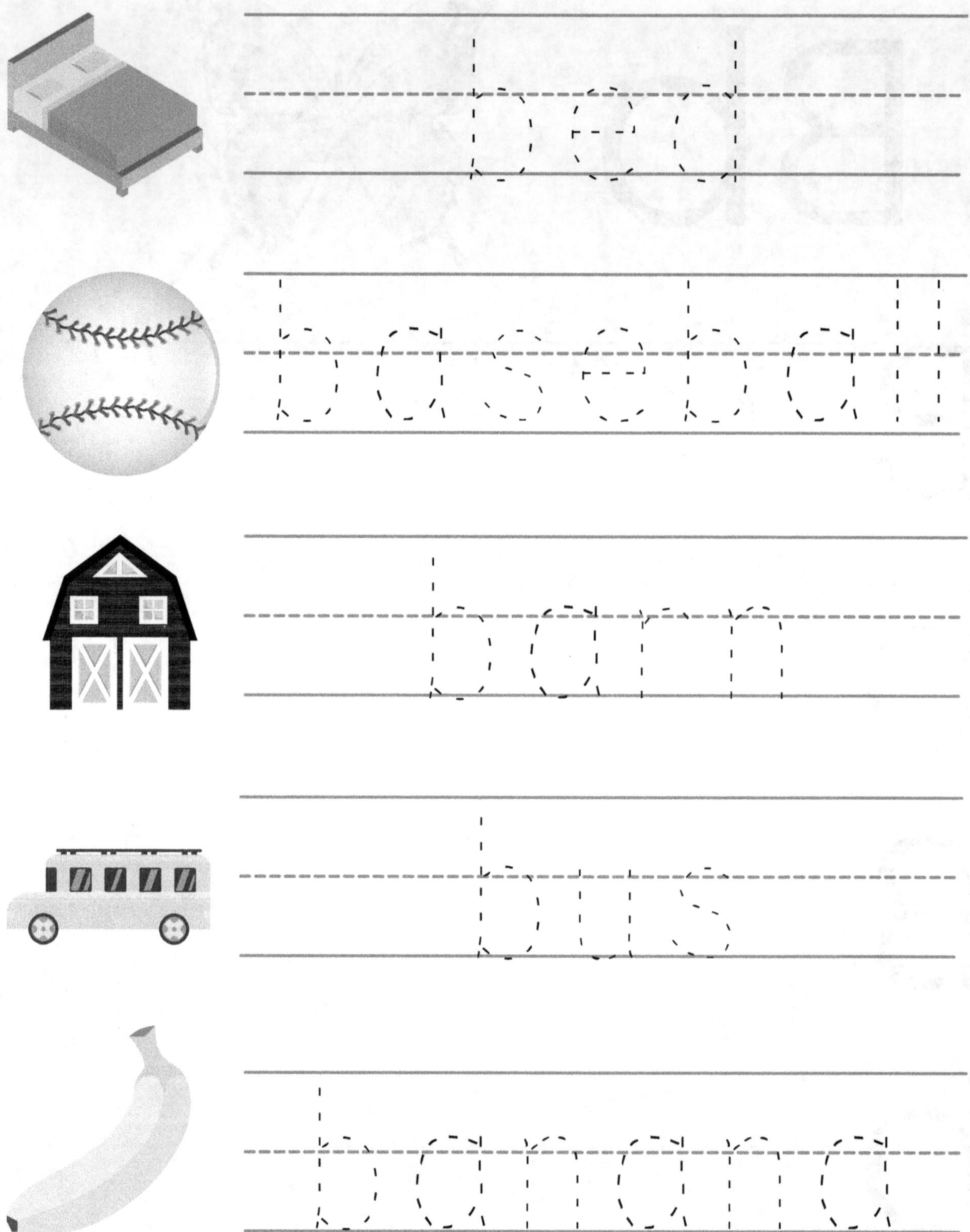

FIND THE LETTERS.

DIRECTIONS: TRACE THE LETTERS. THEN COLOR THE
CIRCLES THAT HAVE THE LETTER YOU TRACED.

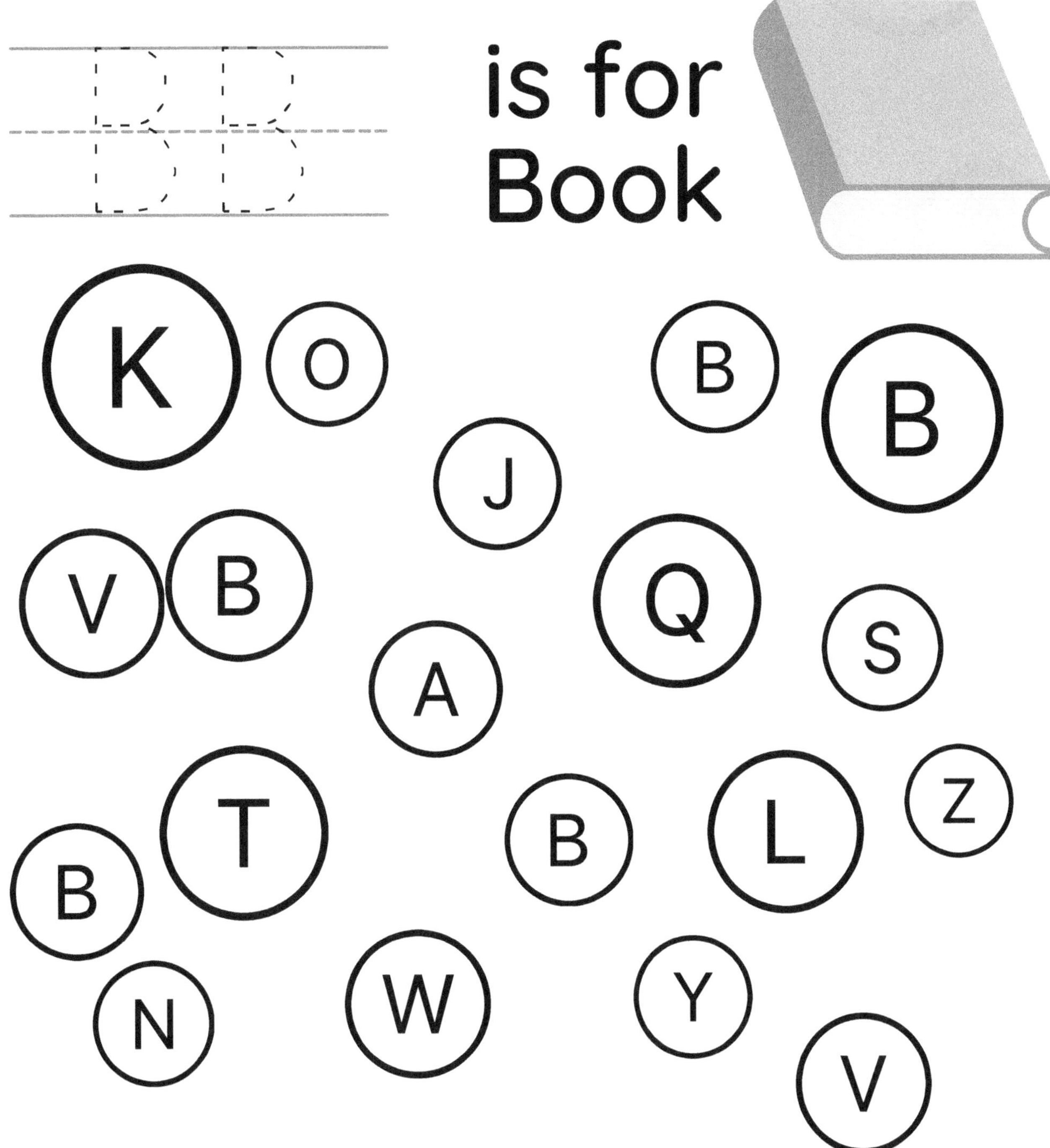

DIRECTIONS: TRACE THE WORDS THAT BEGIN WITH THE LETTER C

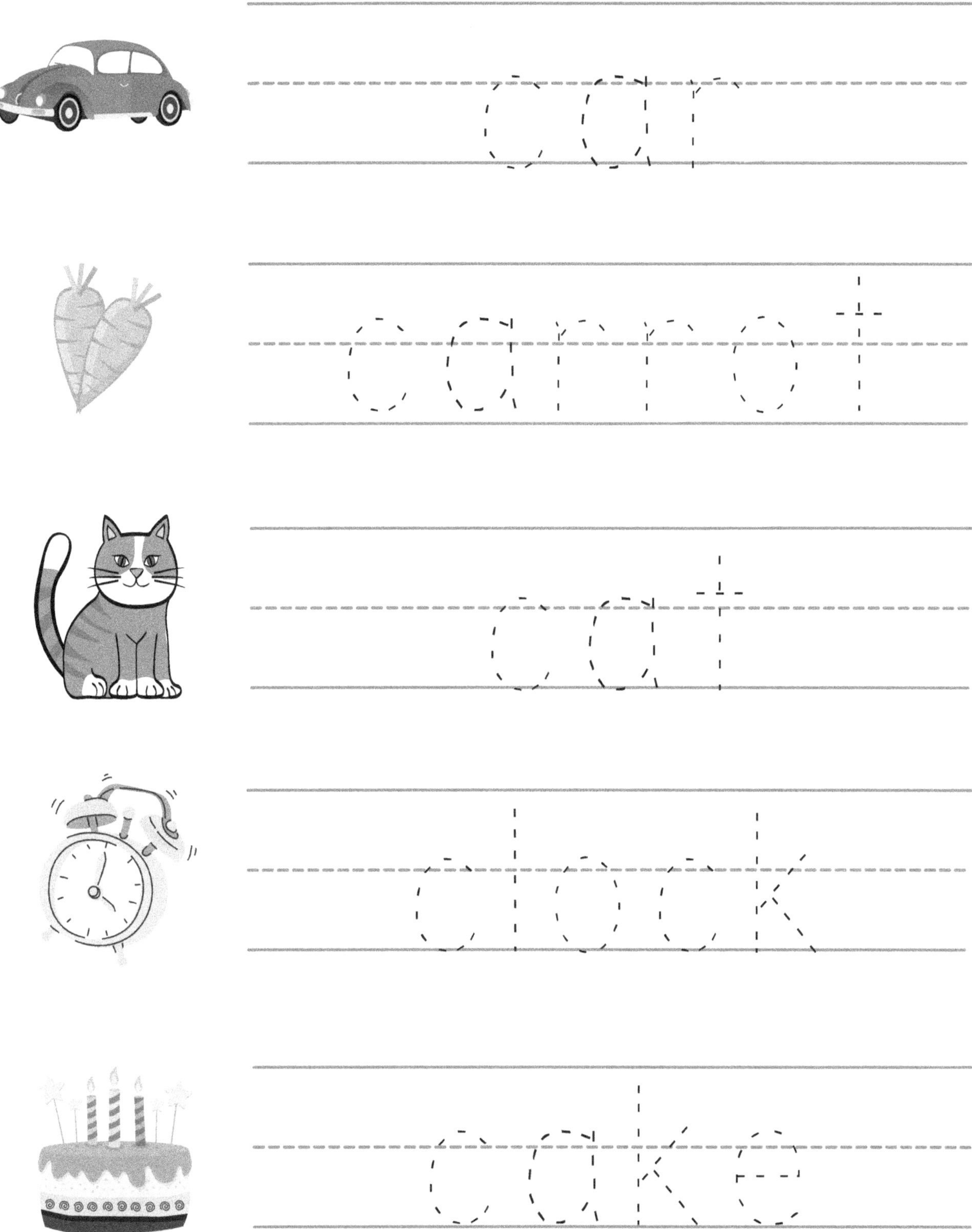

FIND THE LETTERS.

DIRECTIONS: TRACE THE LETTERS. THEN COLOR THE
CIRCLES THAT HAVE THE LETTER YOU TRACED.

is for
Cat

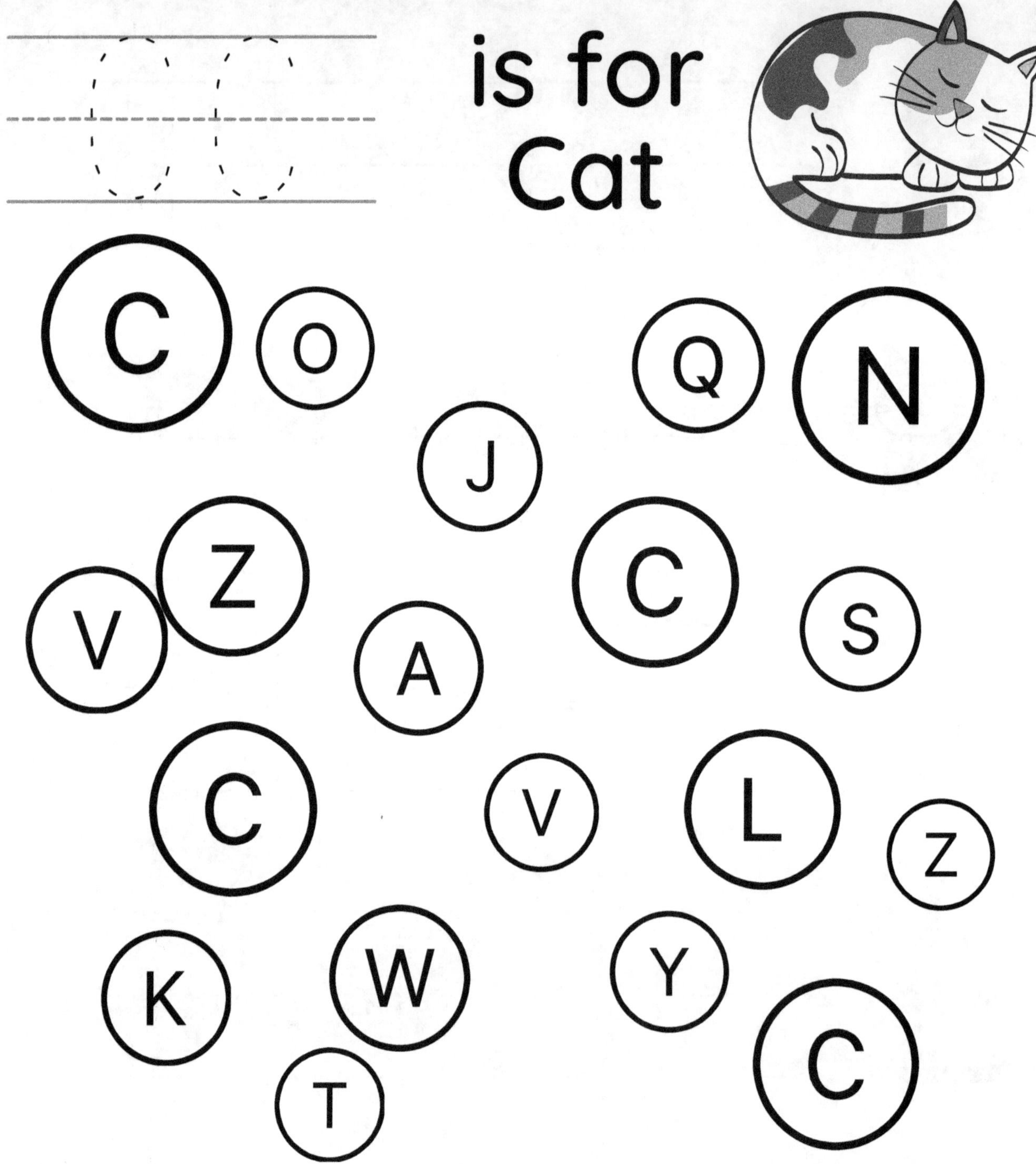

DIRECTIONS: PRACTICE WRITING EACH LETTER IN THE SPACE PROVIDED.

Dd

DIRECTIONS: TRACE THE WORDS THAT BEGIN WITH THE LETTER D

FIND THE LETTERS.

DIRECTIONS: TRACE THE LETTERS. THEN COLOR THE
CIRCLES THAT HAVE THE LETTER YOU TRACED.

is for
Dog

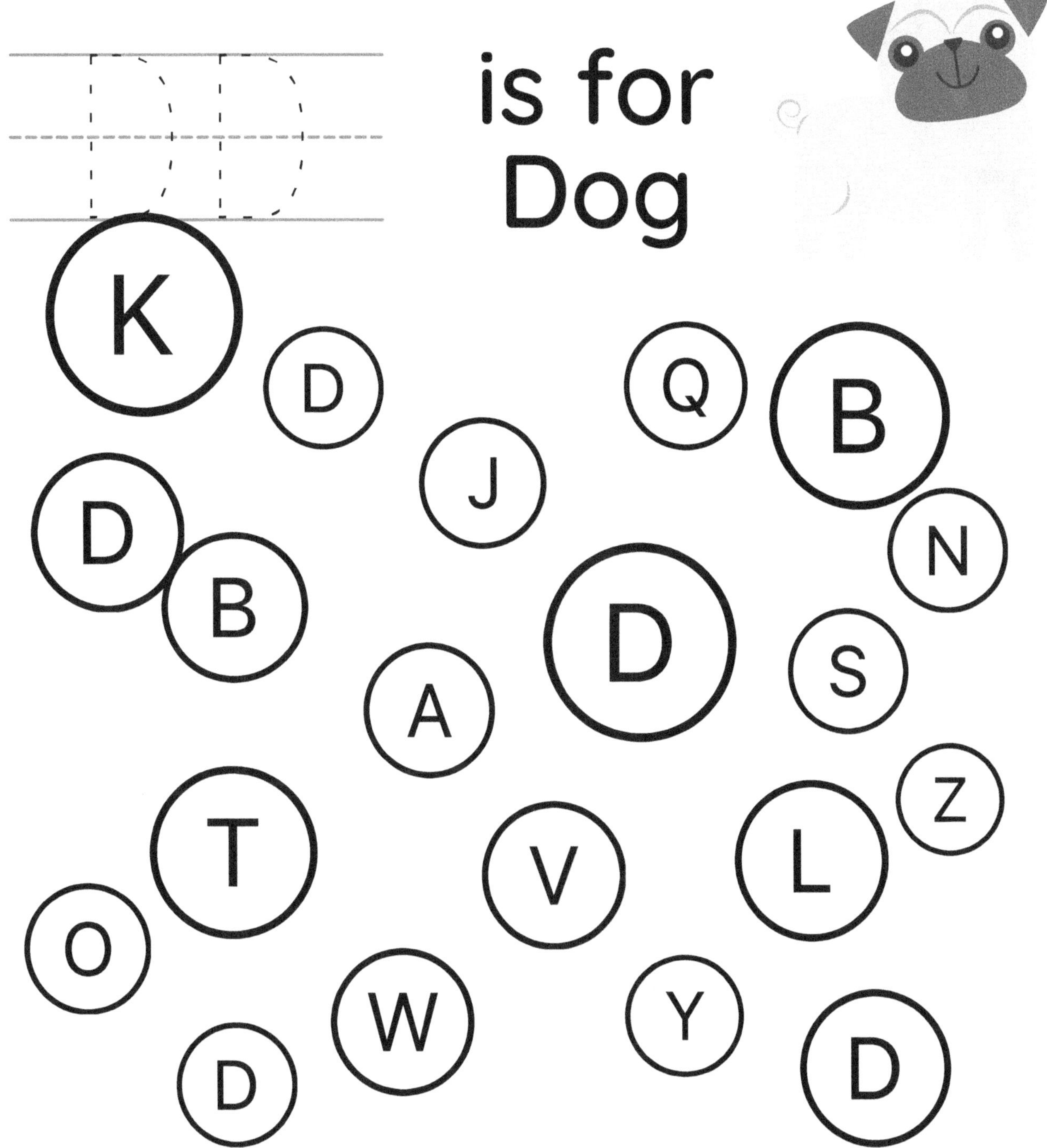

DIRECTIONS: PRACTICE WRITING EACH LETTER IN THE SPACE PROVIDED.

E e

DIRECTIONS: TRACE THE WORDS THAT BEGIN WITH THE LETTER E

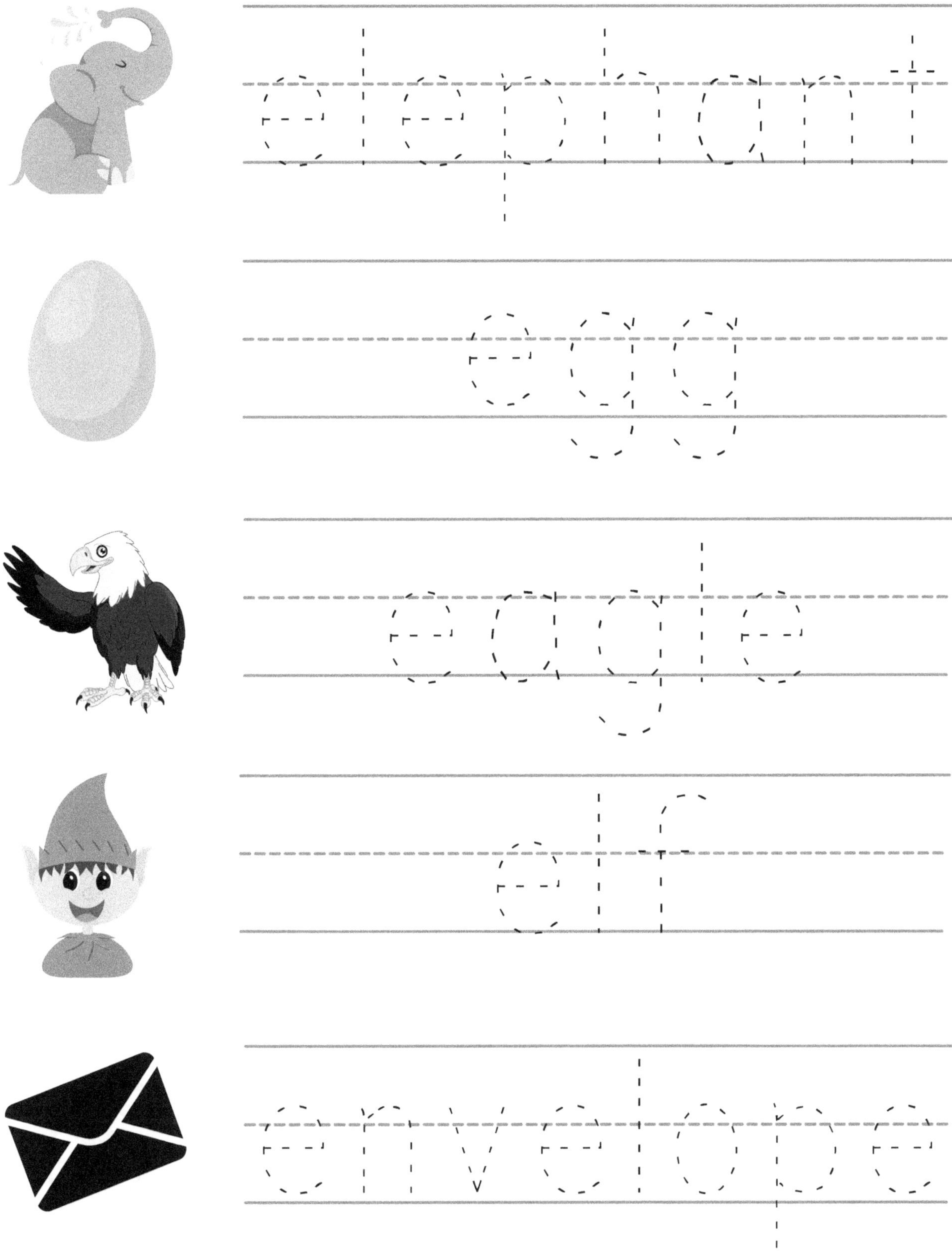

FIND THE LETTERS.

DIRECTIONS: TRACE THE LETTERS. THEN COLOR THE
CIRCLES THAT HAVE THE LETTER YOU TRACED.

is for
Egg

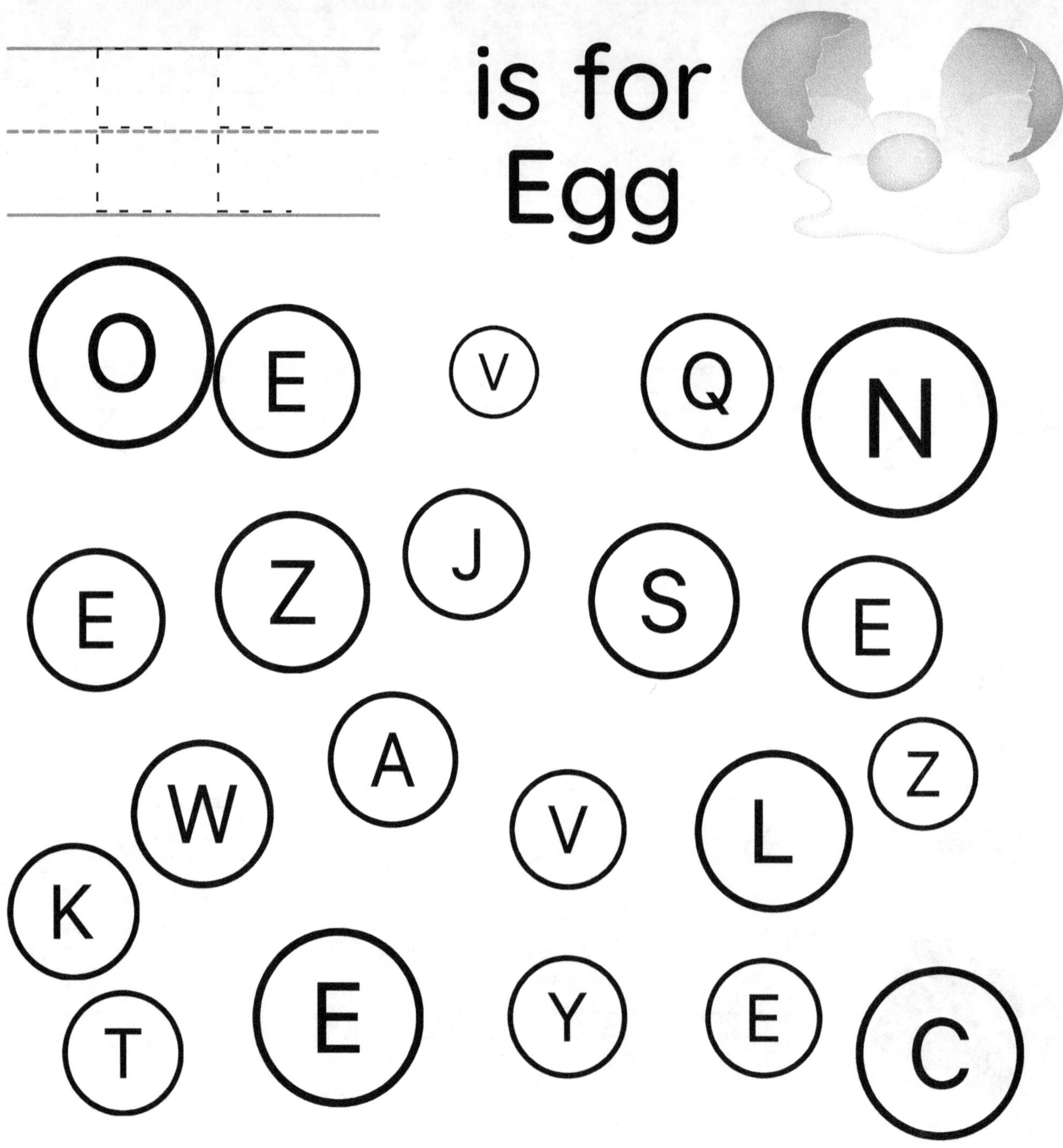

Directions : practice writtinging each letter in the space provided

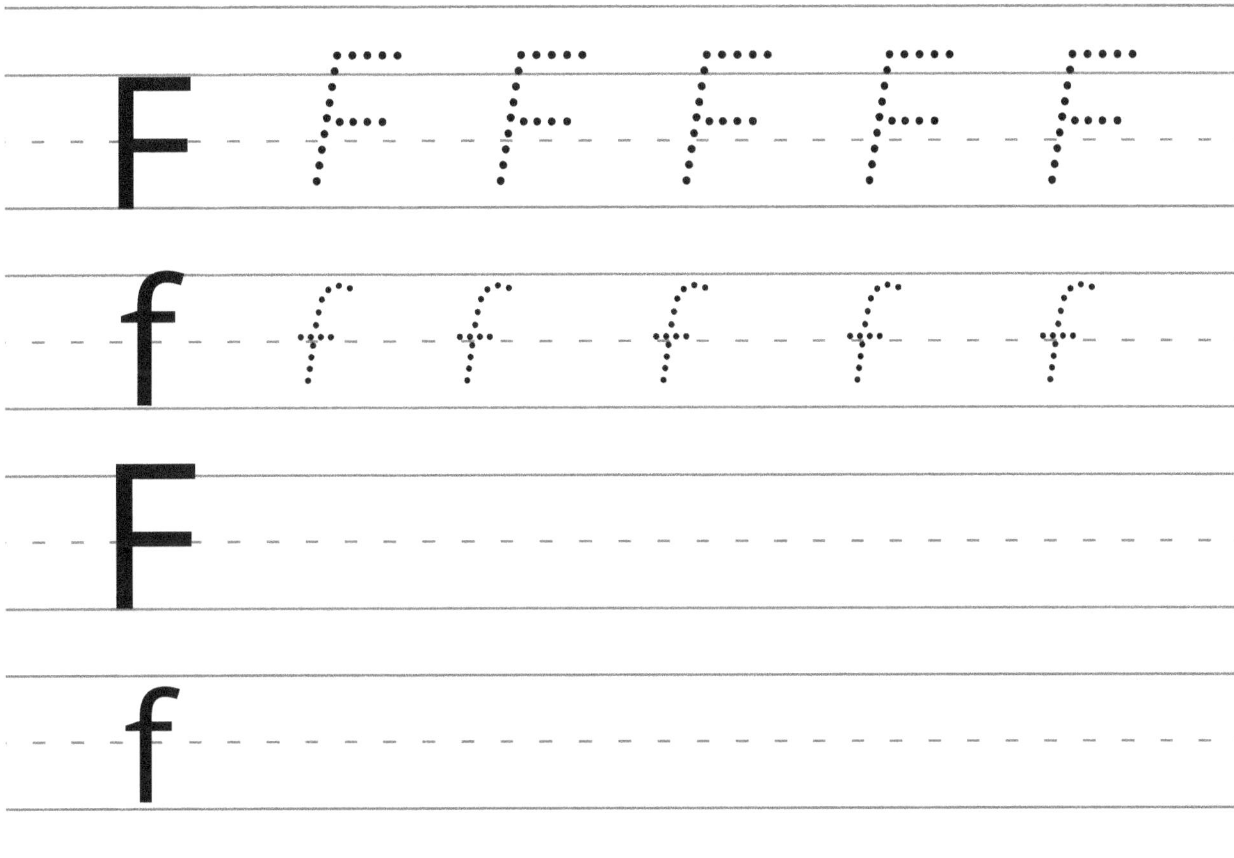

DIRECTIONS: TRACE THE WORDS THAT BEGIN WITH THE LETTER F

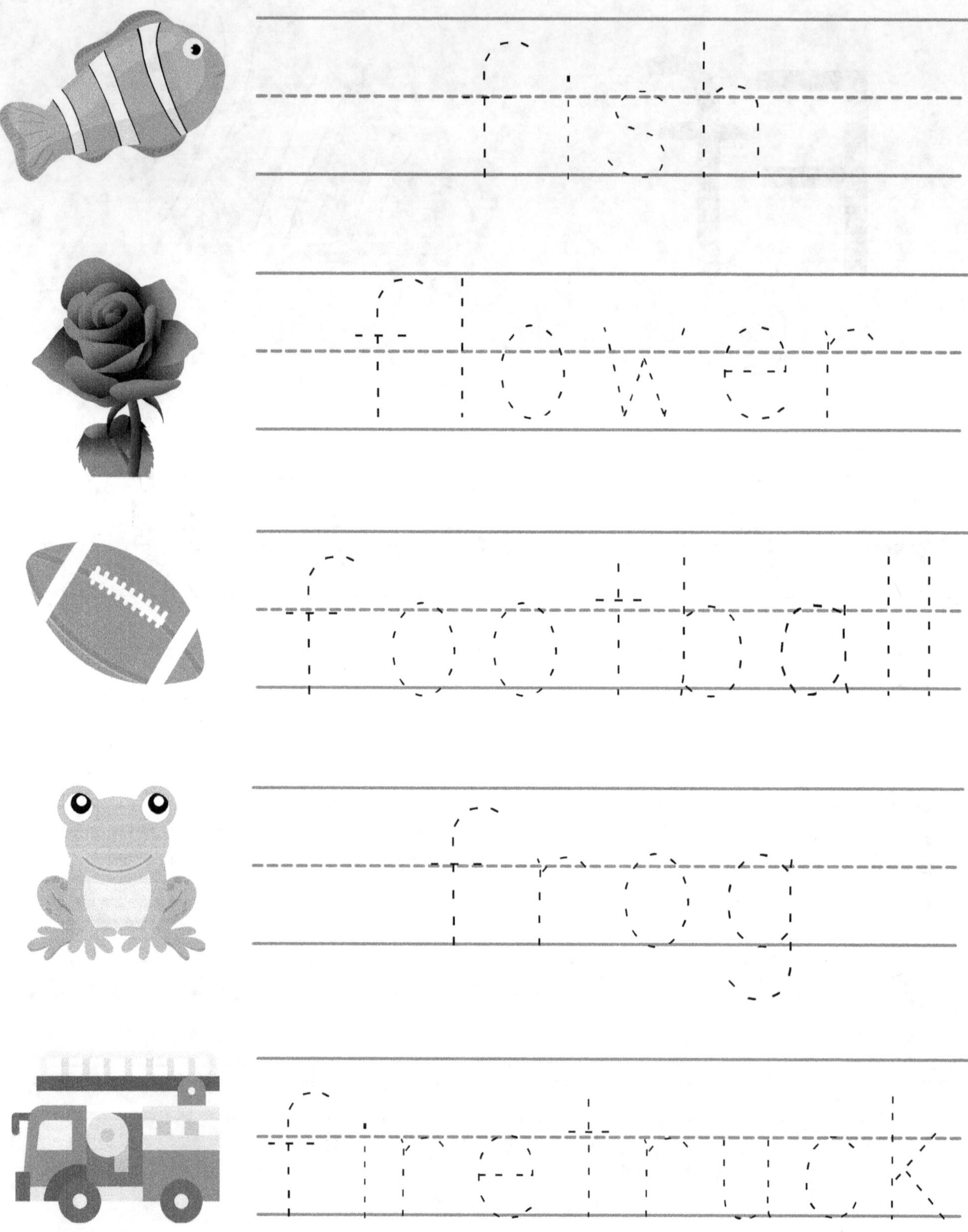

FIND THE LETTERS.

G is for

Gg Gg Gg Gg Gg

Gg Gg Gg Gg Gg

Go Go Go Go Go

Get Get Get Get

Got Got Got Got

DIRECTIONS: TRACE THE WORDS THAT BEGIN WITH THE LETTER G

glasses

goat

girl

giraffe

guitar

FIND THE LETTERS.

DIRECTIONS: TRACE THE LETTERS. THEN COLOR THE CIRCLES THAT HAVE THE LETTER YOU TRACED.

is for Grass

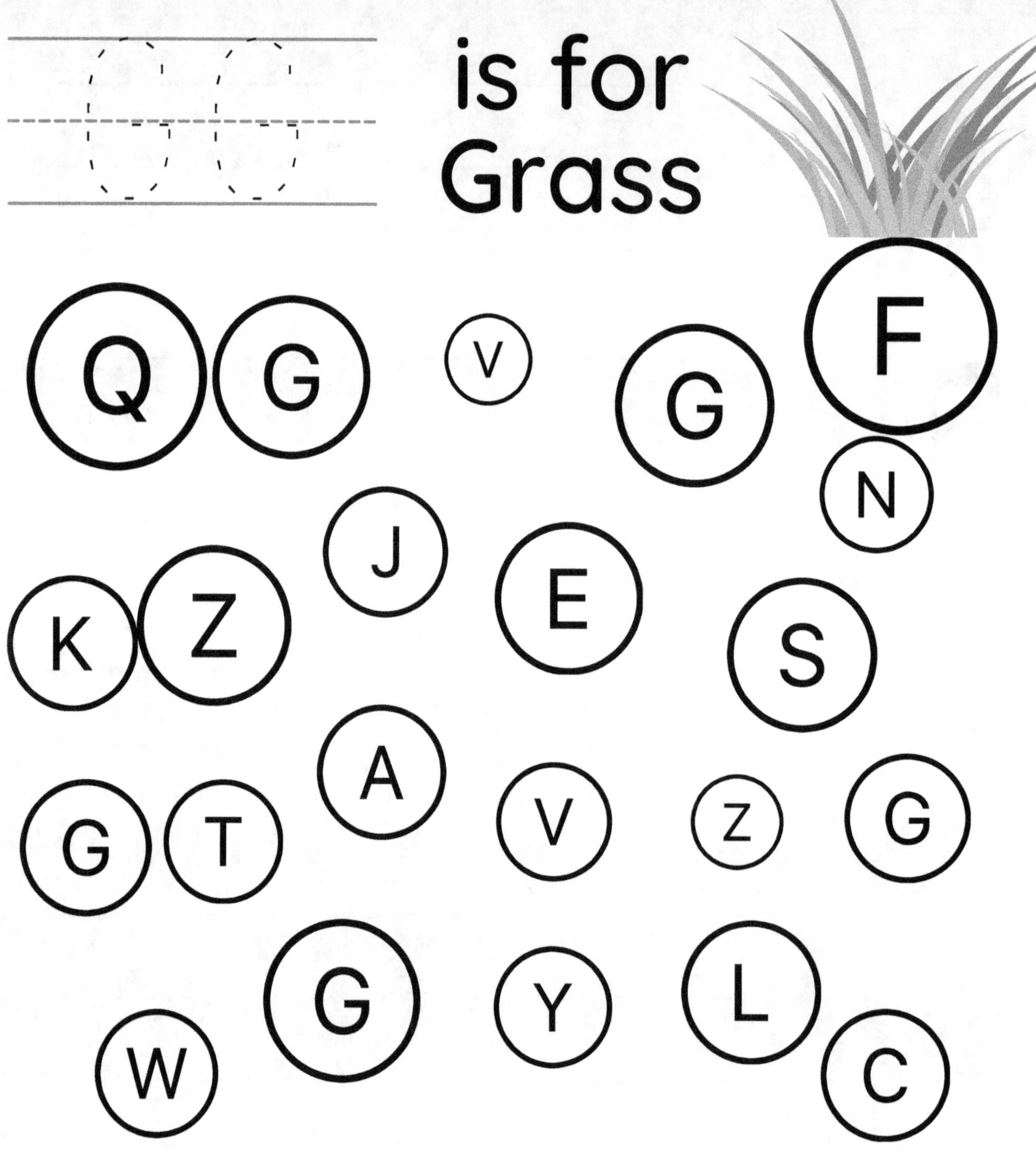

H is for

Hh Hh Hh Hh Hh

Hh Hh Hh Hh Hh

Hi Hi Hi Hi Hi Hi

Hat Hat Hat Hat

Hop Hop Hop

DIRECTIONS: TRACE THE WORDS THAT BEGIN WITH THE LETTER H

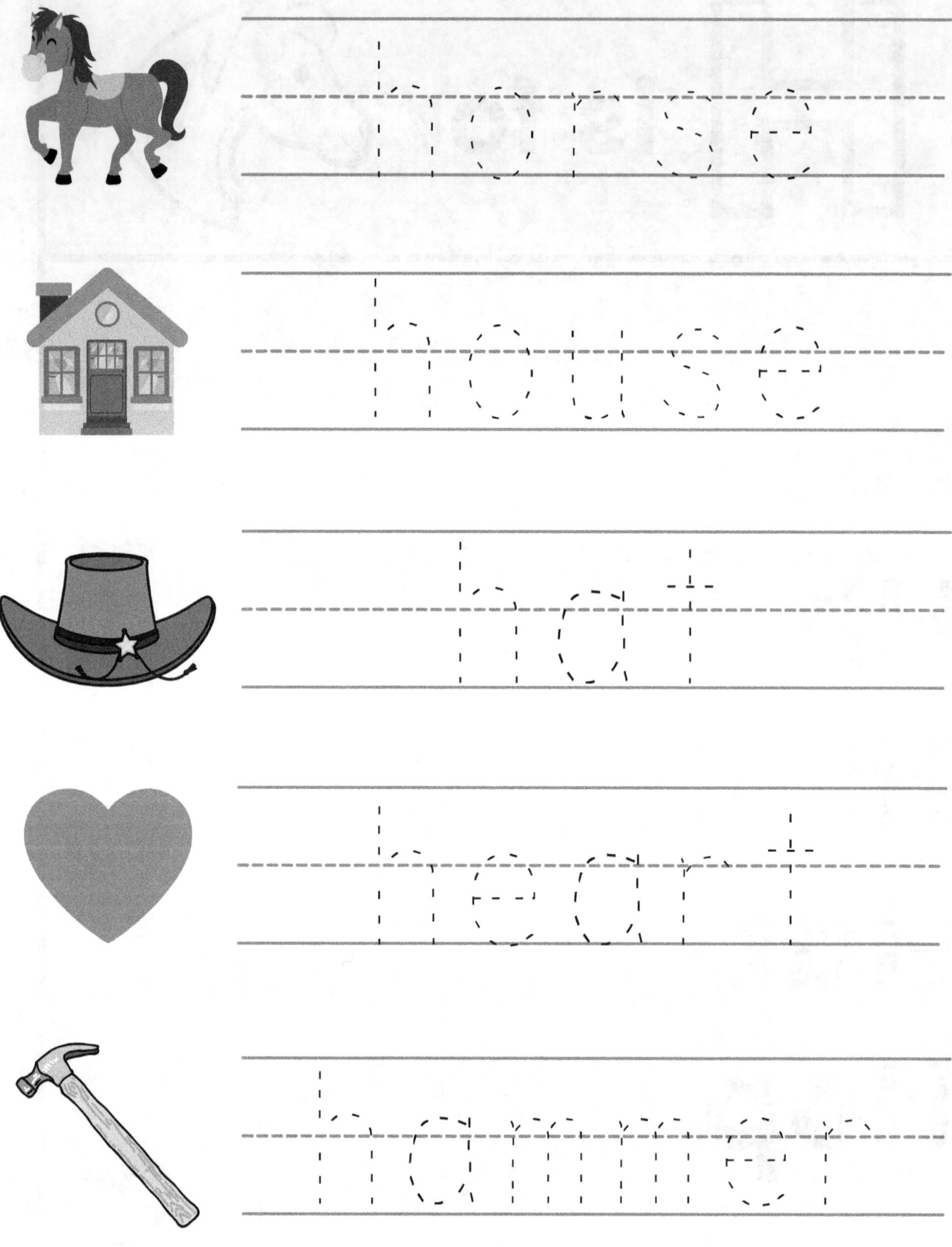

FIND THE LETTERS.

DIRECTIONS: TRACE THE LETTERS. THEN COLOR THE
CIRCLES THAT HAVE THE LETTER YOU TRACED.

is for
Hen

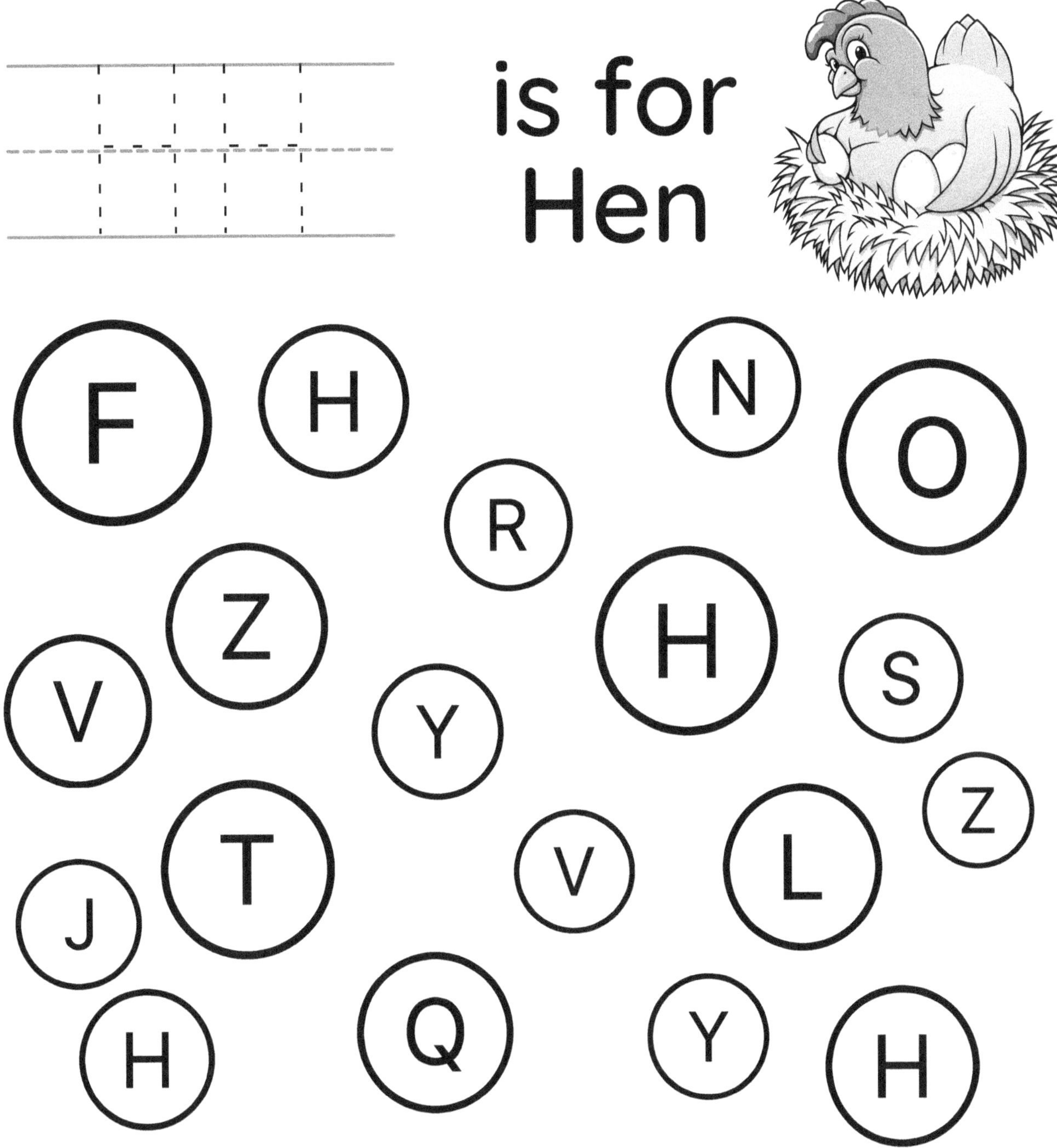

Practise your uppercase and lowercase Is below:

Trace these words that begin with the letter I:

DIRECTIONS: TRACE THE WORDS THAT BEGIN WITH THE LETTER I

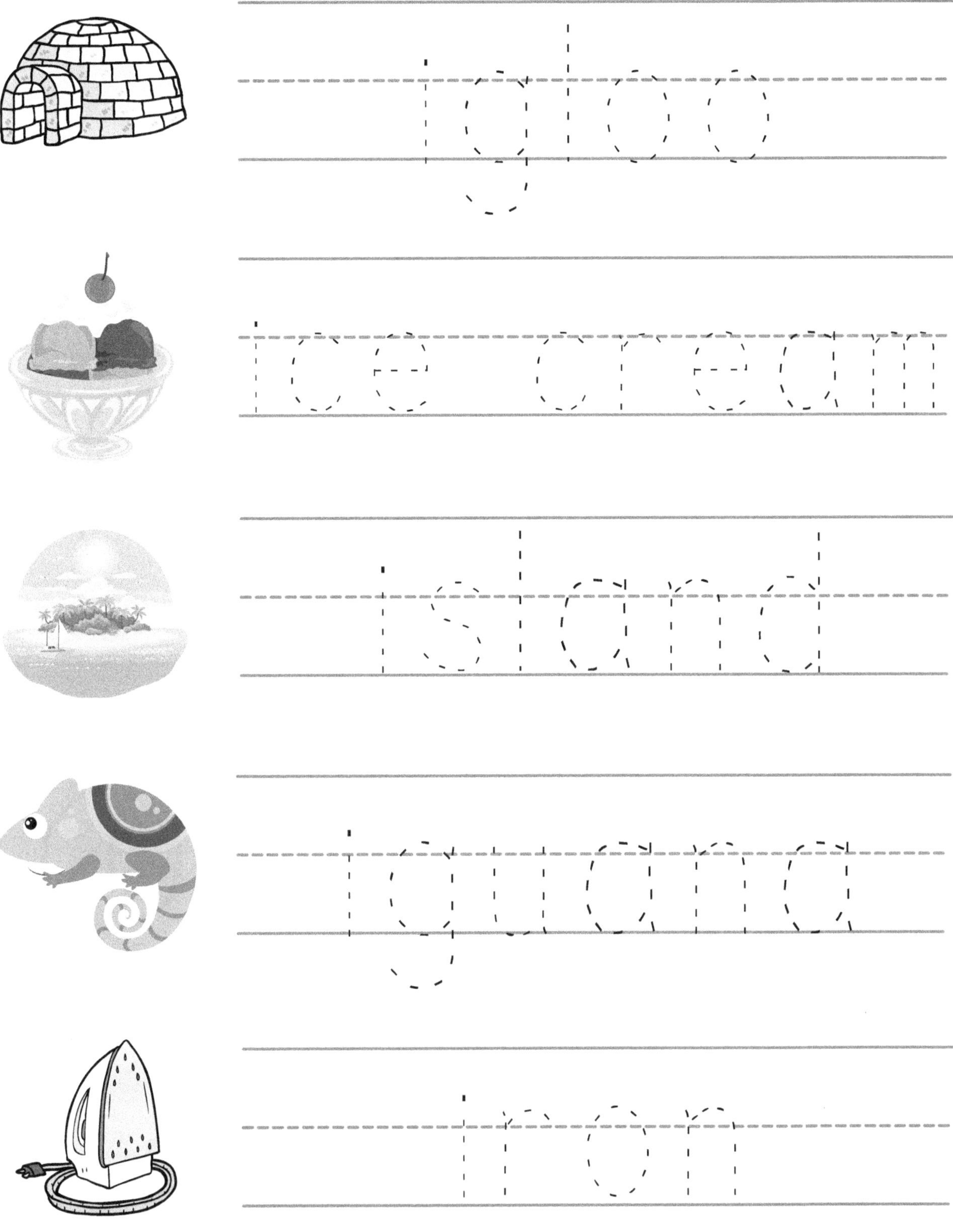

FIND THE LETTERS.

DIRECTIONS: TRACE THE LETTERS. THEN COLOR THE CIRCLES THAT HAVE THE LETTER YOU TRACED.

is for
Igloo

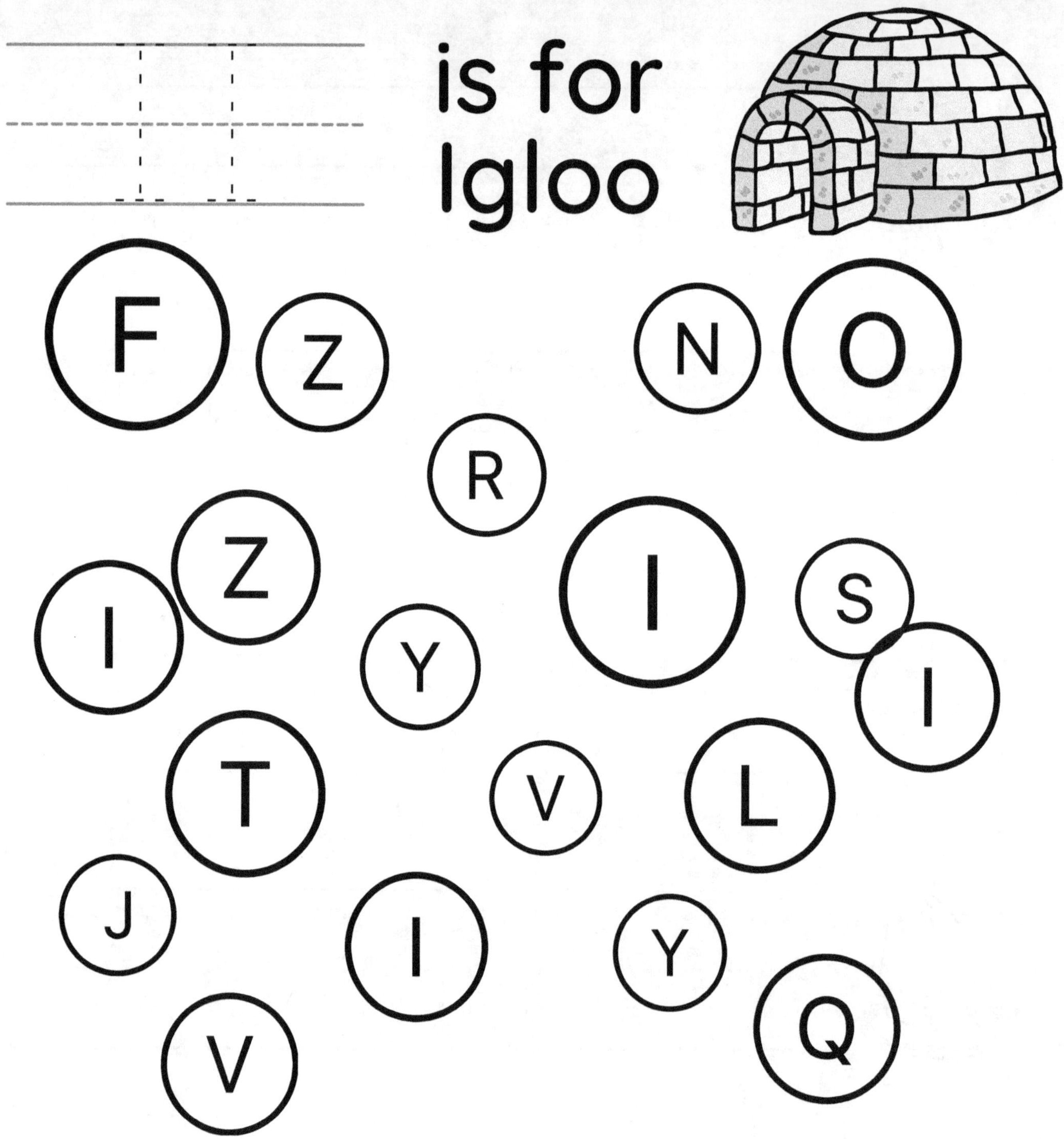

Jj

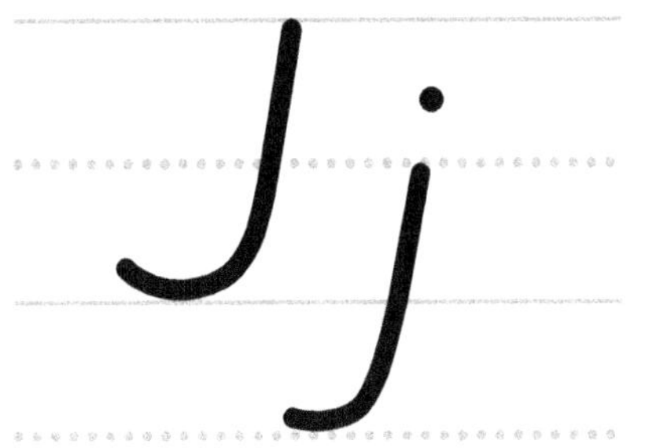

Jellyfish

J

j

Jj

Jug

Jelly

Jewel

Jacket

DIRECTIONS: TRACE THE WORDS THAT BEGIN WITH THE LETTER J

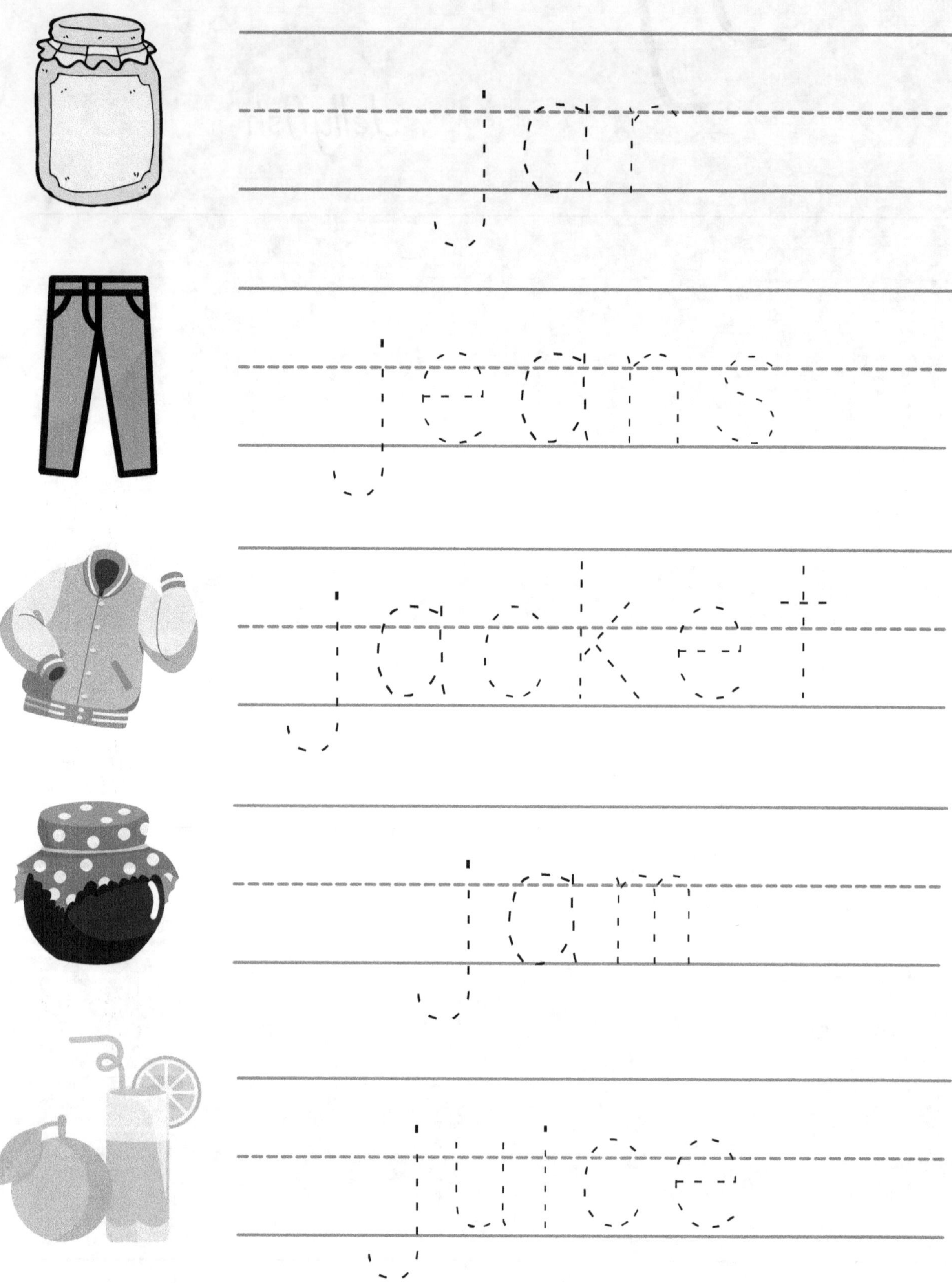

FIND THE LETTERS.

DIRECTIONS: TRACE THE LETTERS. THEN COLOR THE
CIRCLES THAT HAVE THE LETTER YOU TRACED.

is for
Jar

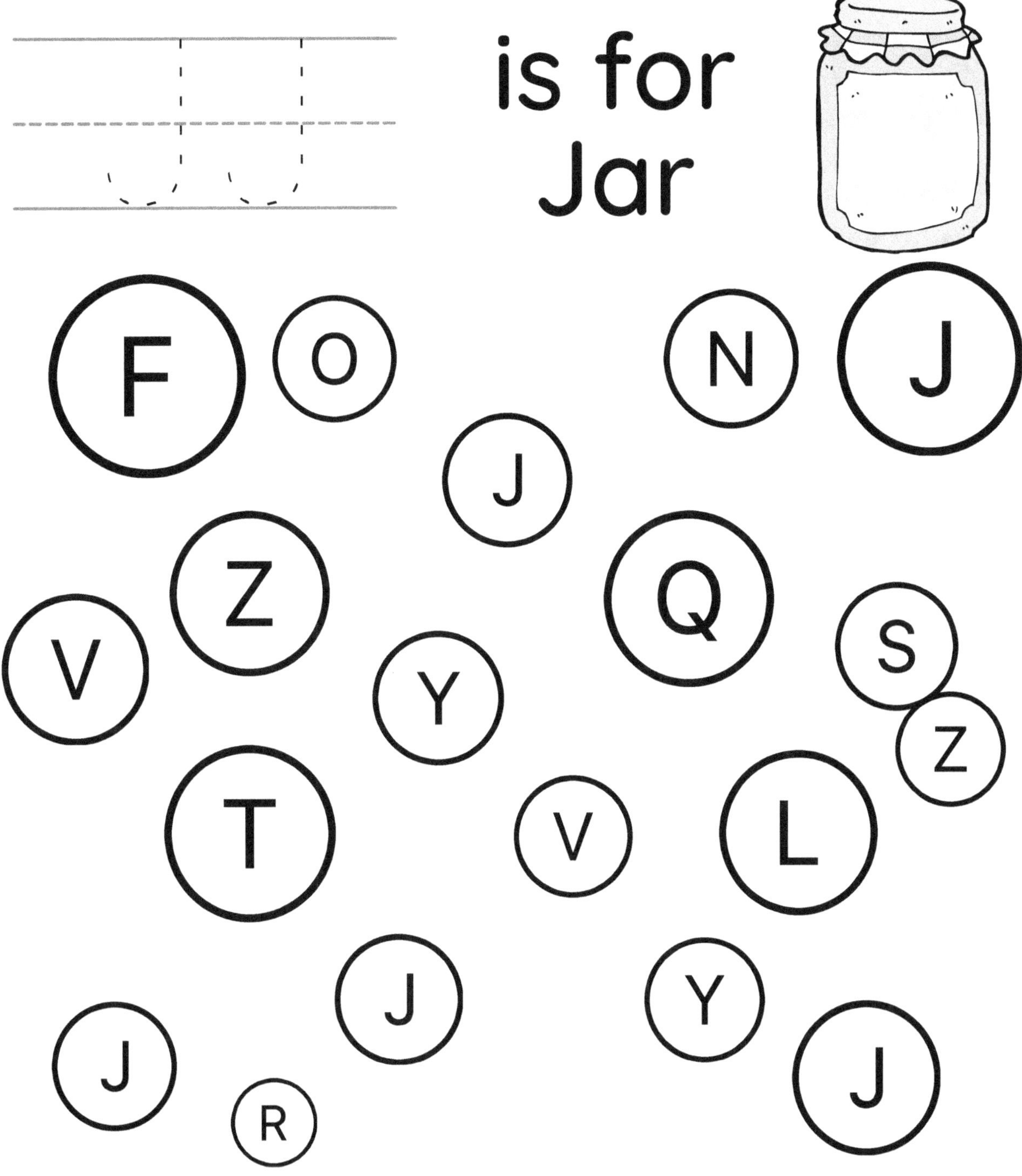

The Letter...

K k

K k __ __ __

K k __ __ __

Draw three (3) things that start with K

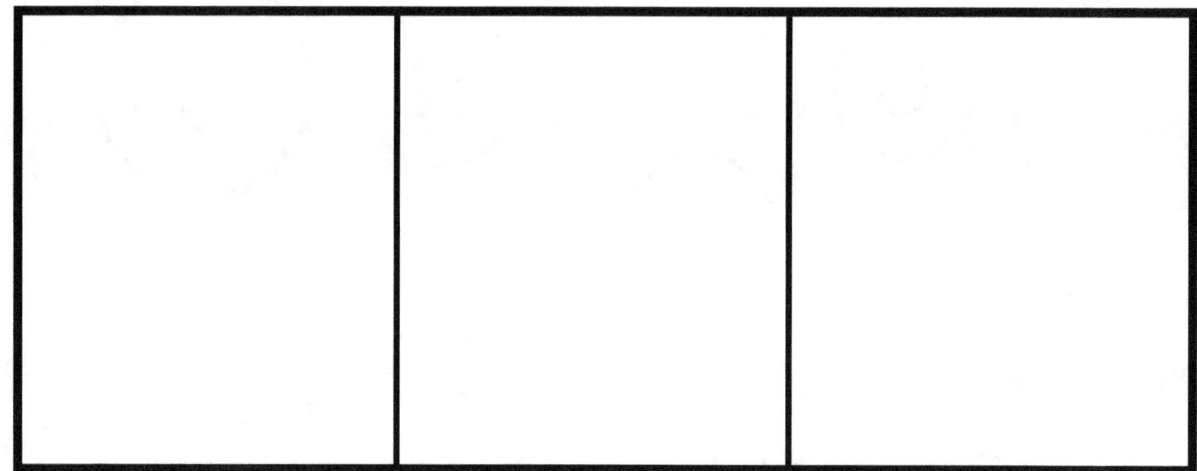

Colour all the letters K, k

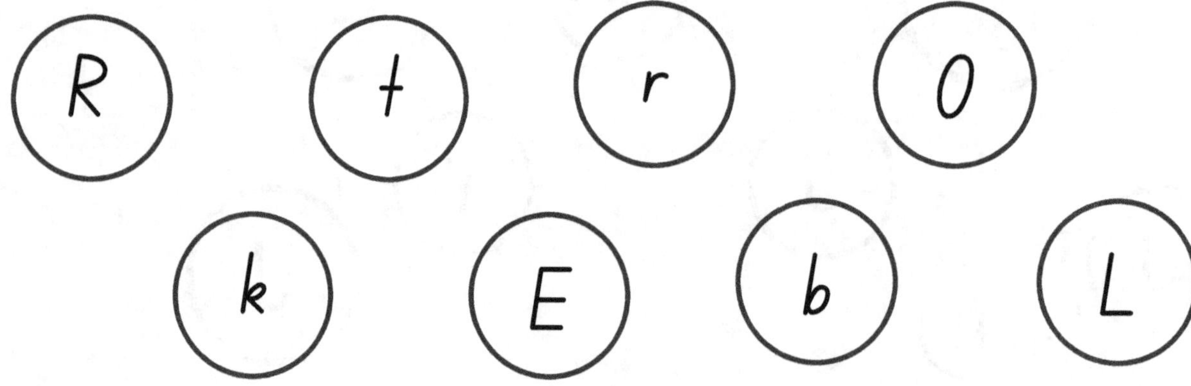

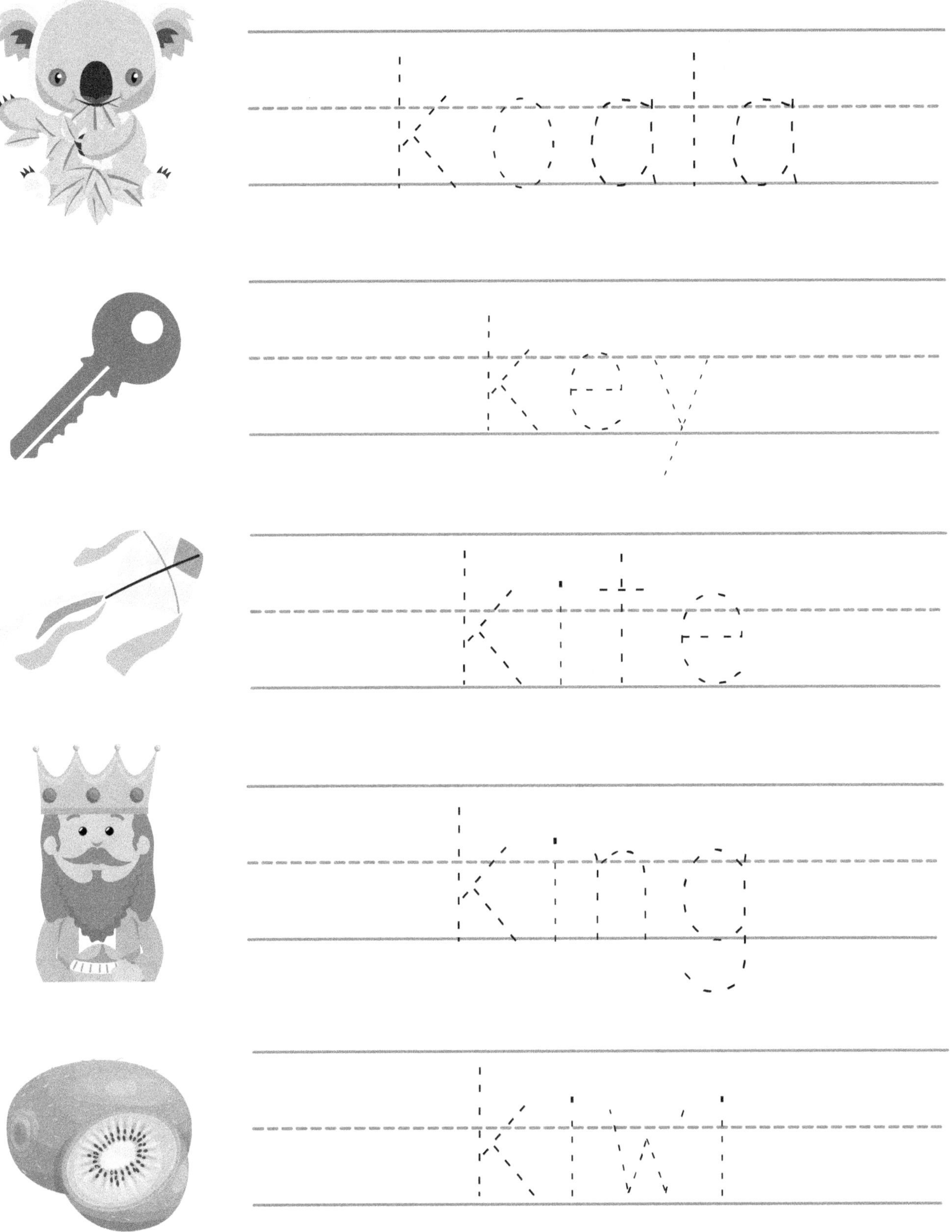

koala
key
kite
king
kiwi

FIND THE LETTERS.

DIRECTIONS: TRACE THE LETTERS. THEN COLOR THE CIRCLES THAT HAVE THE LETTER YOU TRACED.

is for Key

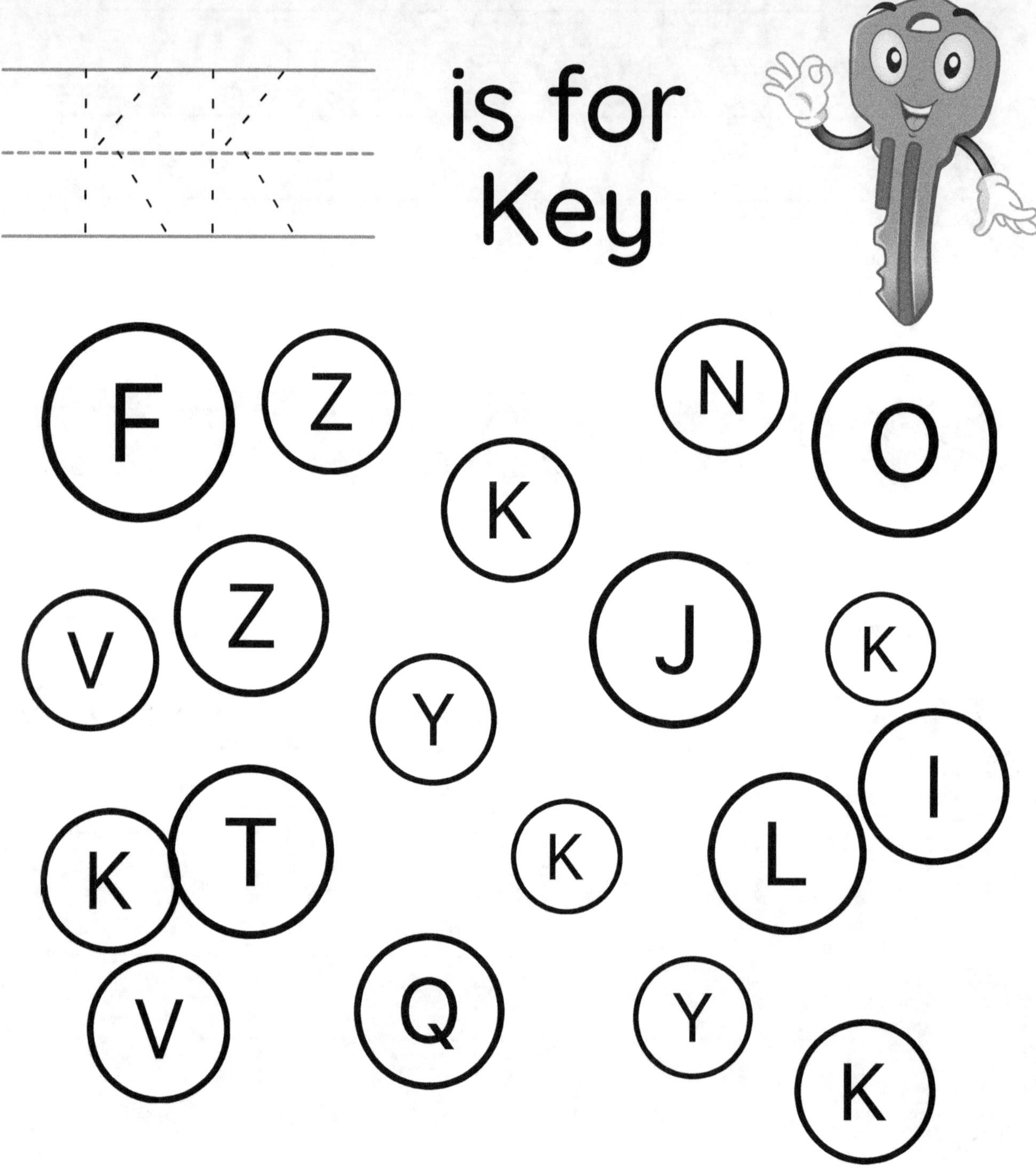

The Letter...

L l ___ ___

Draw three (3) things that start with L

Colour all the letters L, l

DIRECTIONS: TRACE THE WORDS THAT BEGIN WITH THE LETTER L

FIND THE LETTERS.

DIRECTIONS: TRACE THE LETTERS. THEN COLOR THE CIRCLES THAT HAVE THE LETTER YOU TRACED.

is for
Lamp

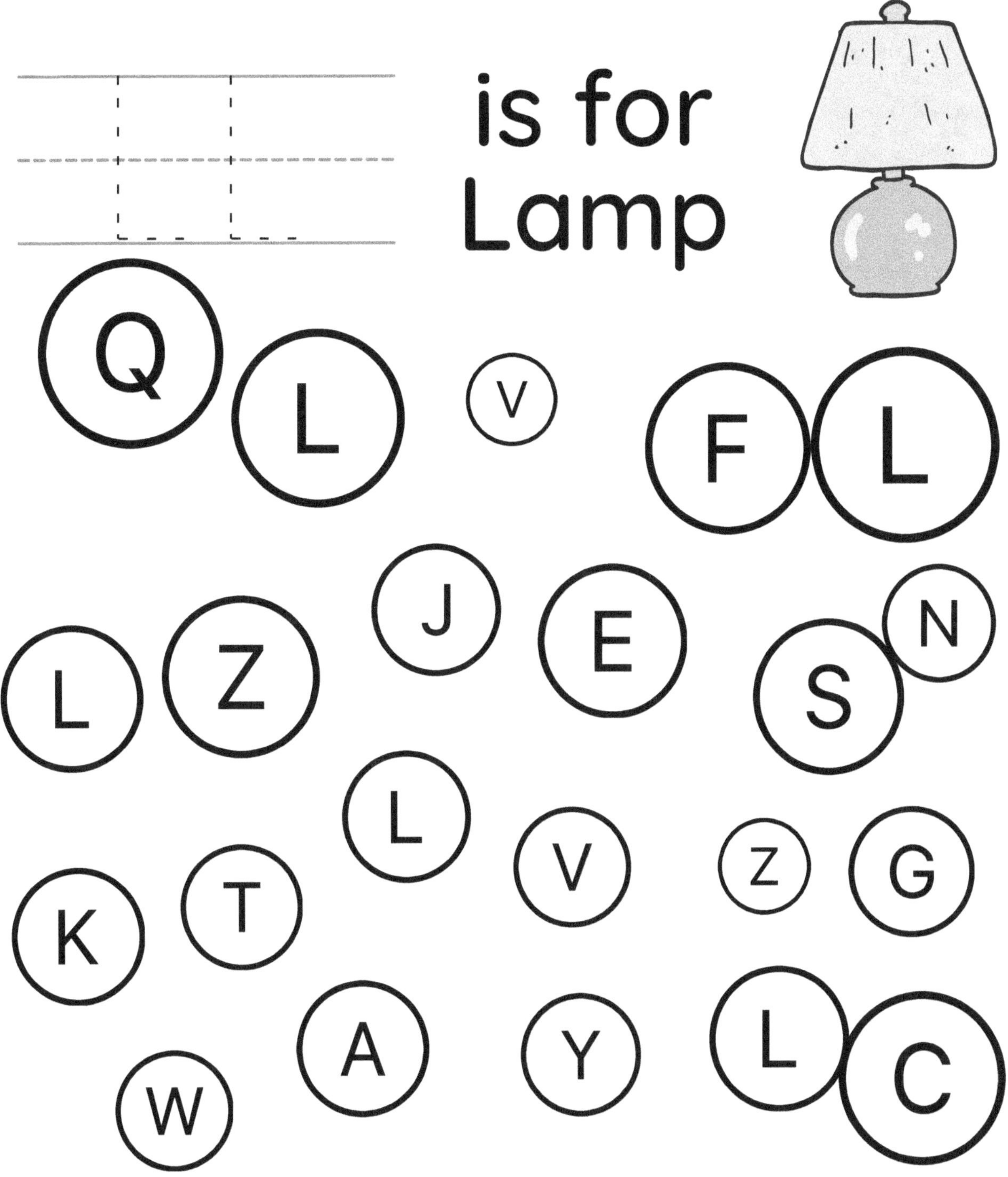

M m

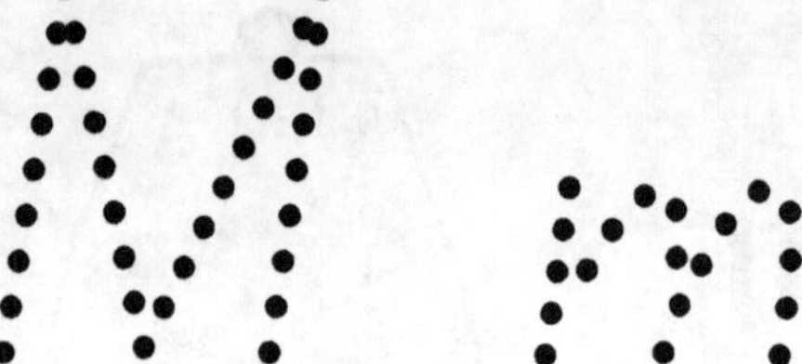

Draw three (3) things that start with M

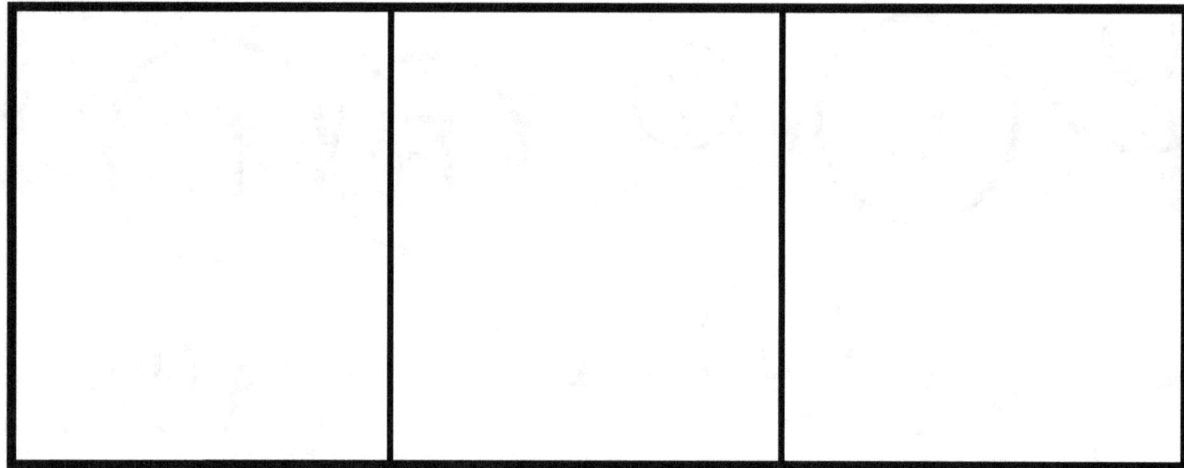

Colour all the letters M, m

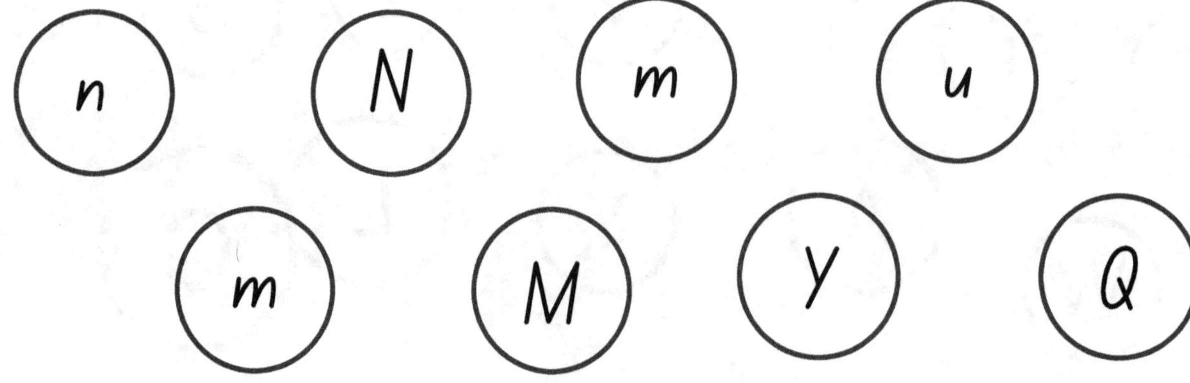

DIRECTIONS: TRACE THE WORDS THAT BEGIN WITH THE LETTER M

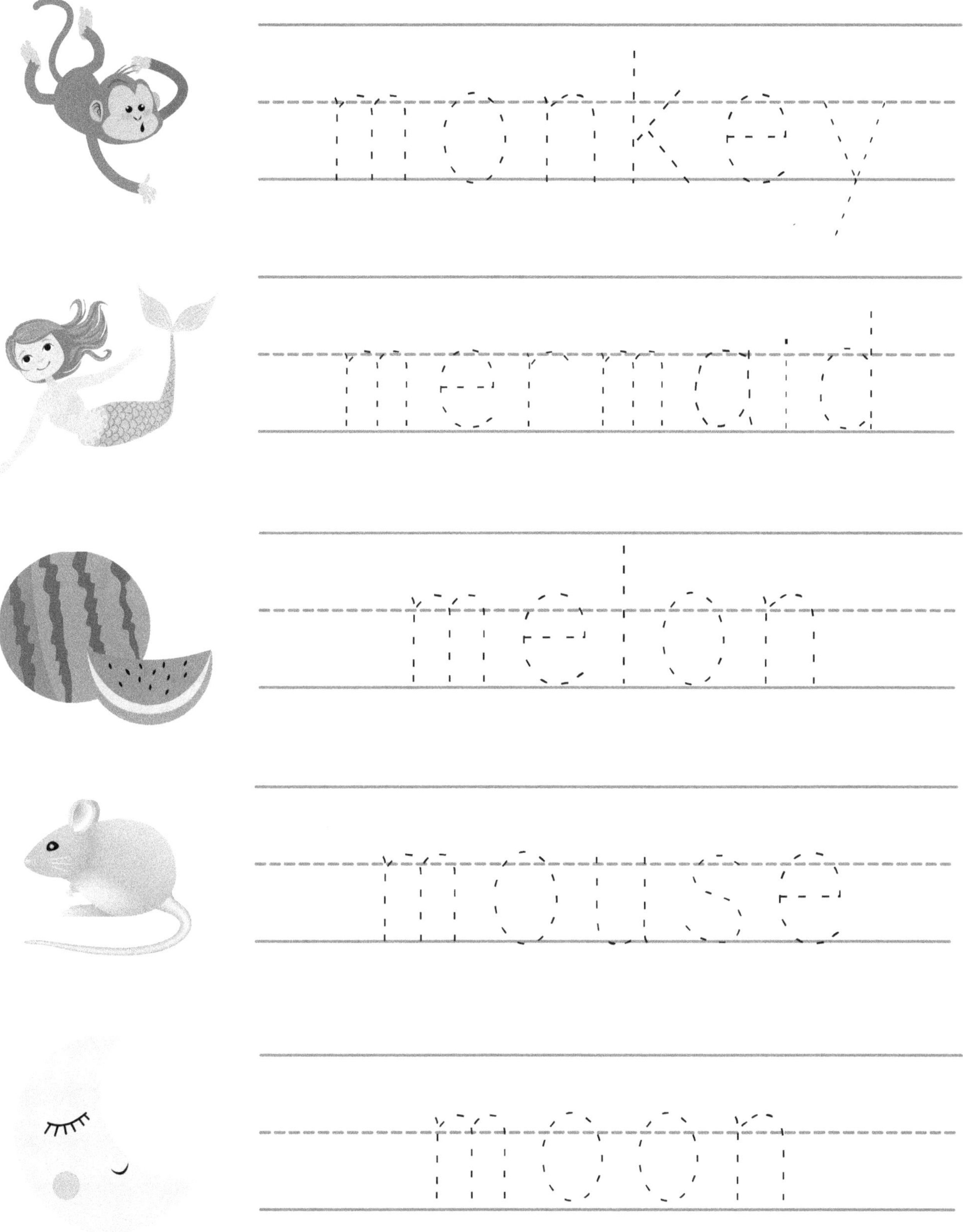

DIRECTIONS: TRACE THE LETTERS. THEN COLOR THE CIRCLES THAT HAVE THE LETTER YOU TRACED.

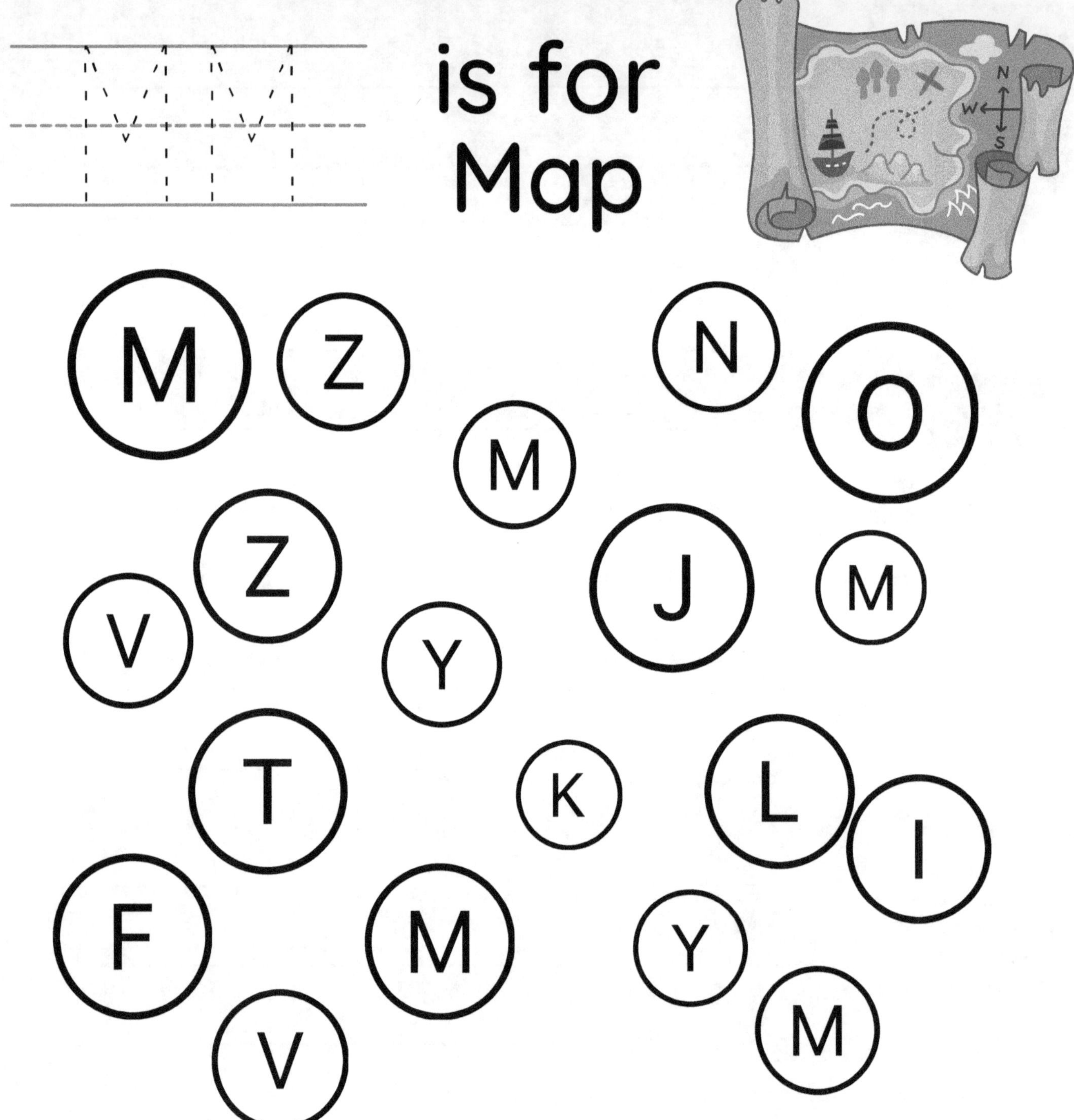

DIRECTIONS: PRACTICE WRITING EACH LETTER IN THE SPACE PROVIDED.

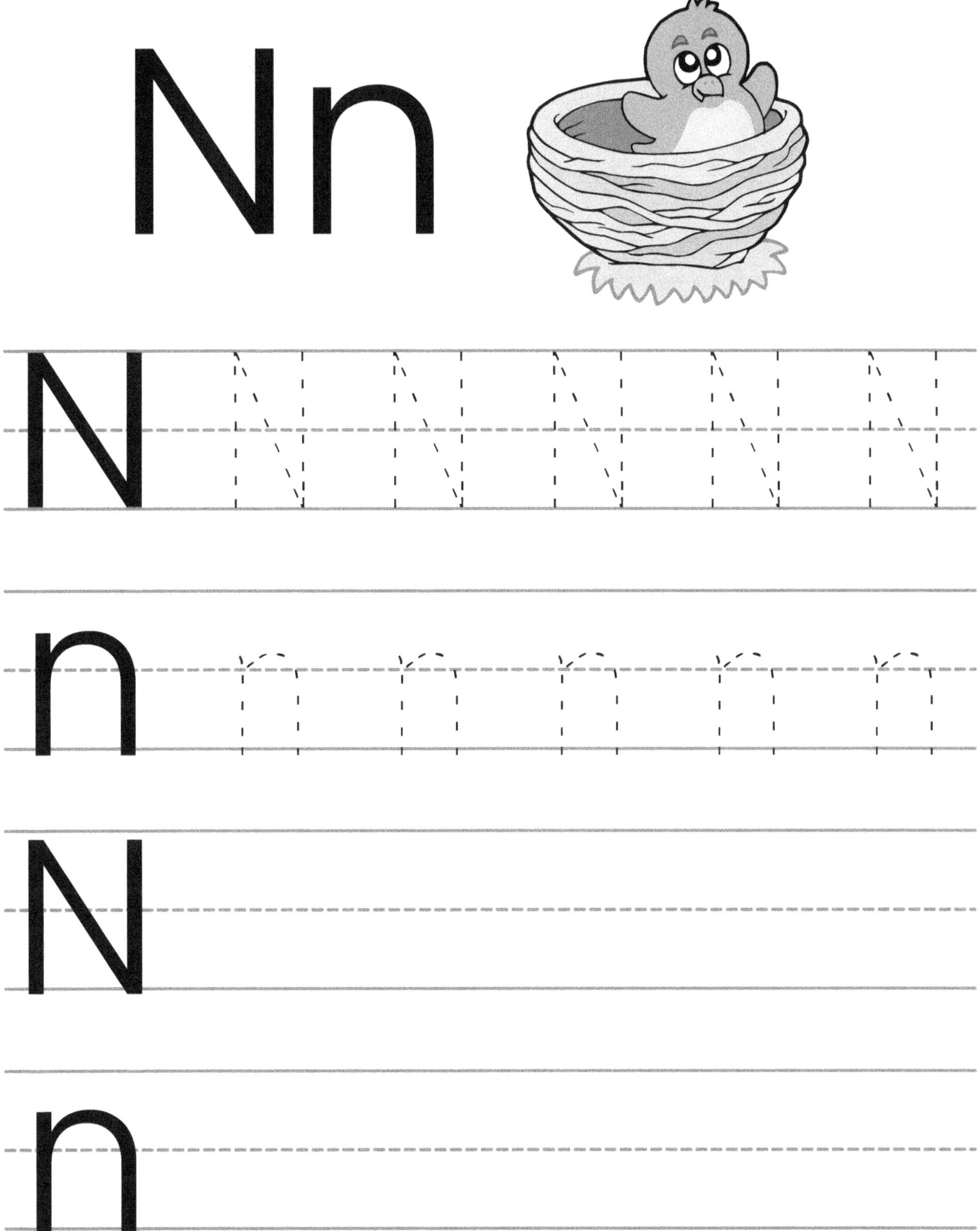

DIRECTIONS: TRACE THE WORDS THAT BEGIN WITH THE LETTER N

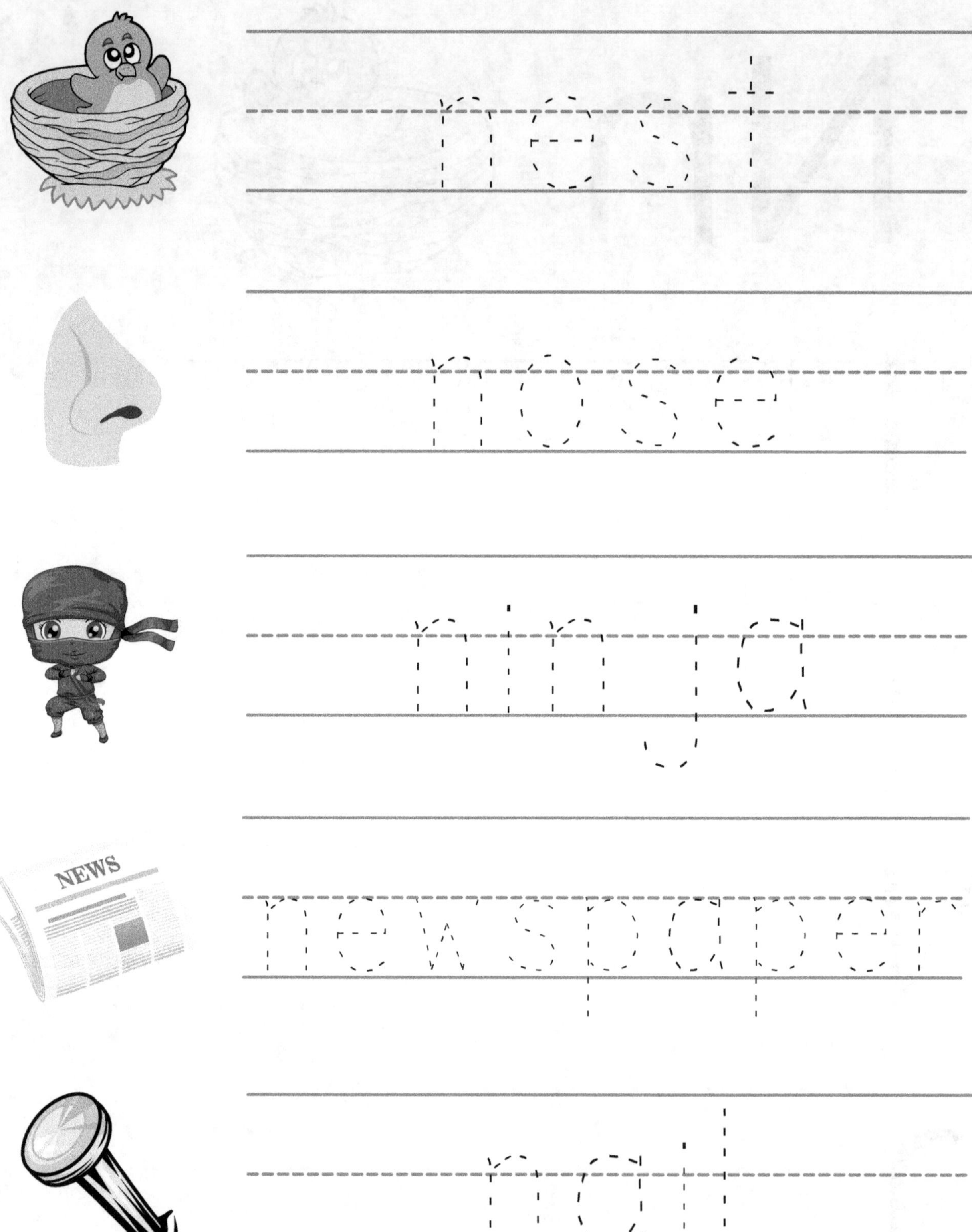

FIND THE LETTERS.

is for
Nurse

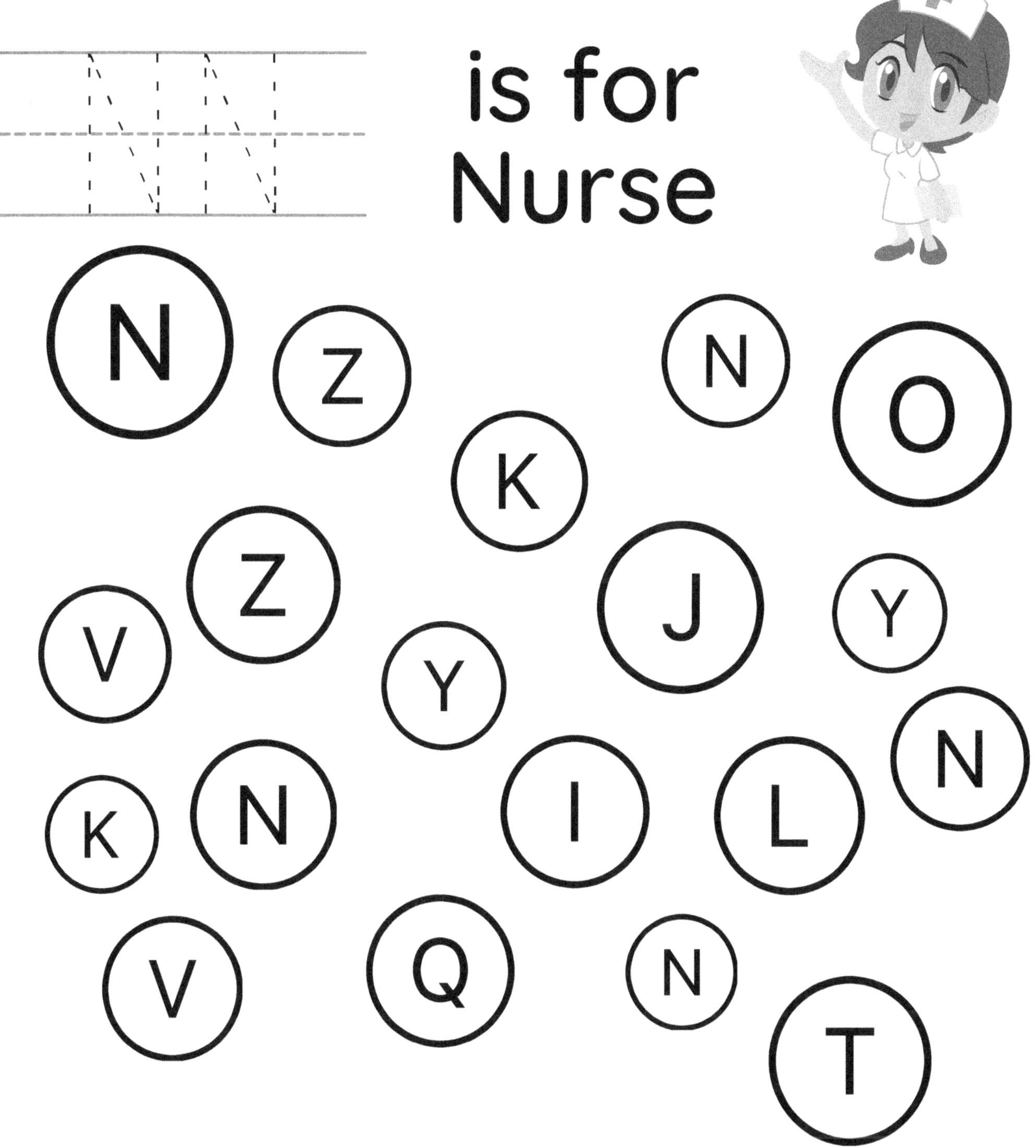

Directions:practice writting the letters in the sspace provided

Oo

DIRECTIONS: TRACE THE WORDS THAT BEGIN WITH THE LETTER O

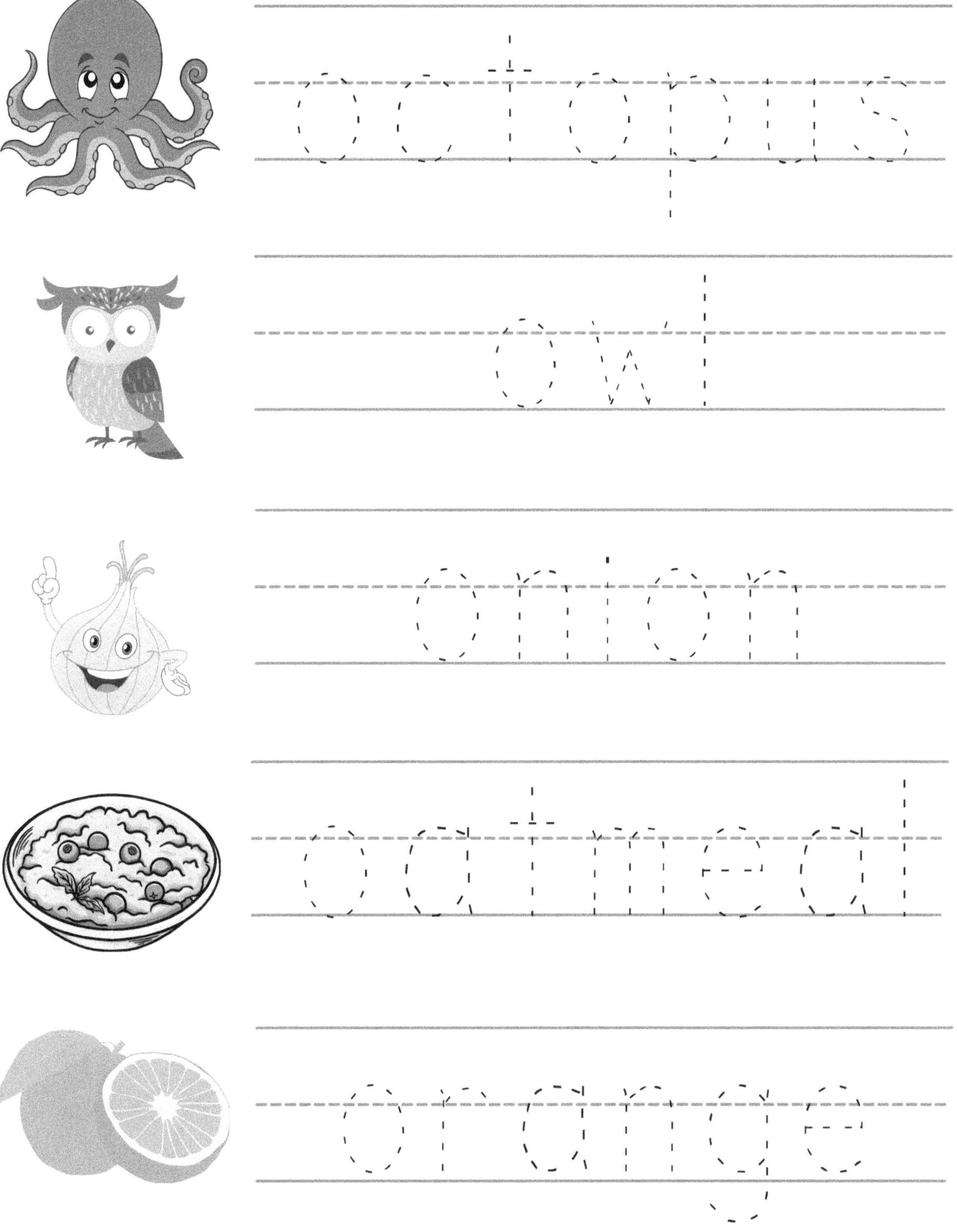

FIND THE LETTERS.

DIRECTIONS: TRACE THE LETTERS. THEN COLOR THE
CIRCLES THAT HAVE THE LETTER YOU TRACED.

is for
Owl

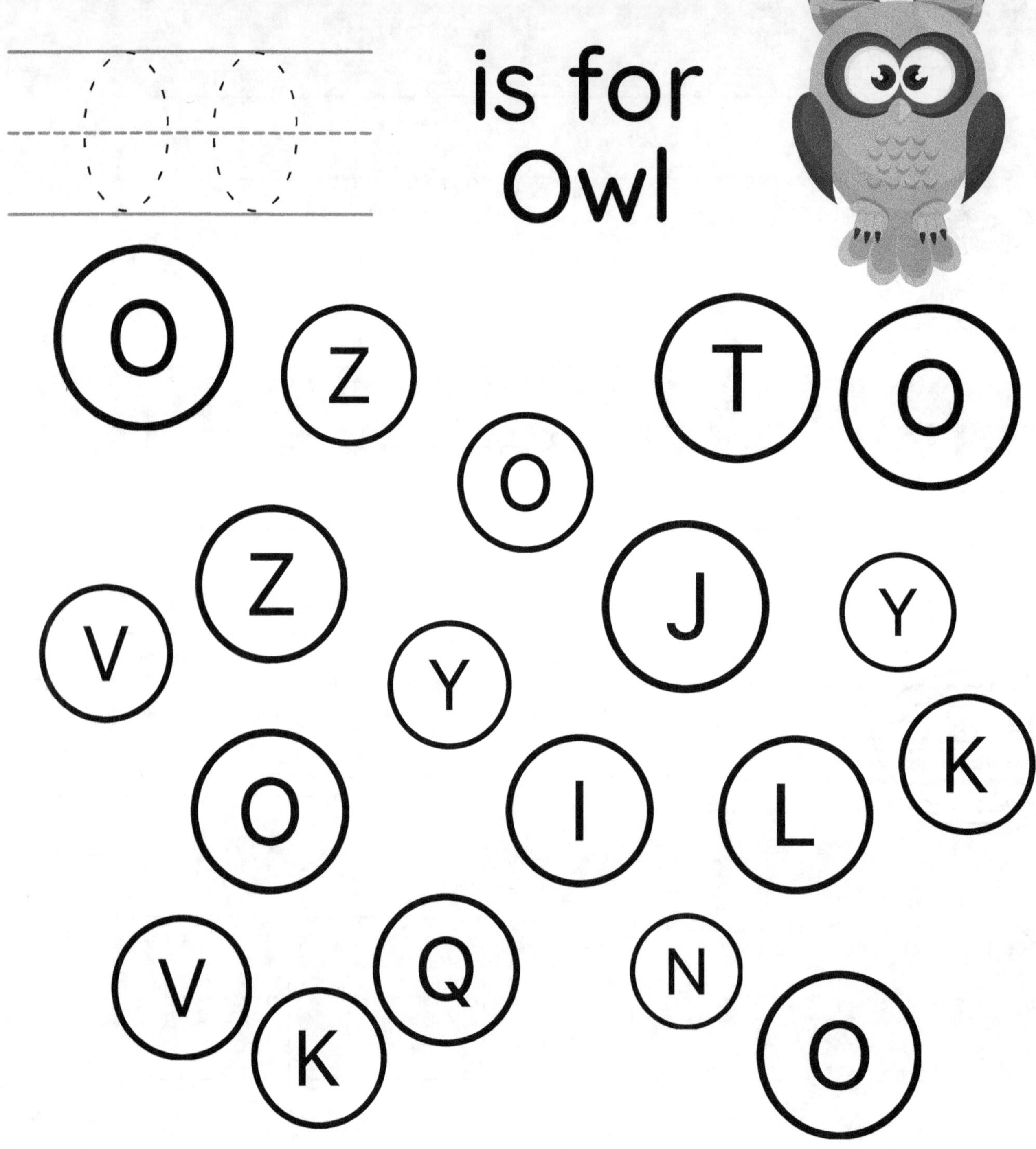

DIRECTIONS: PRACTICE WRITING EACH LETTER IN THE SPACE PROVIDED.

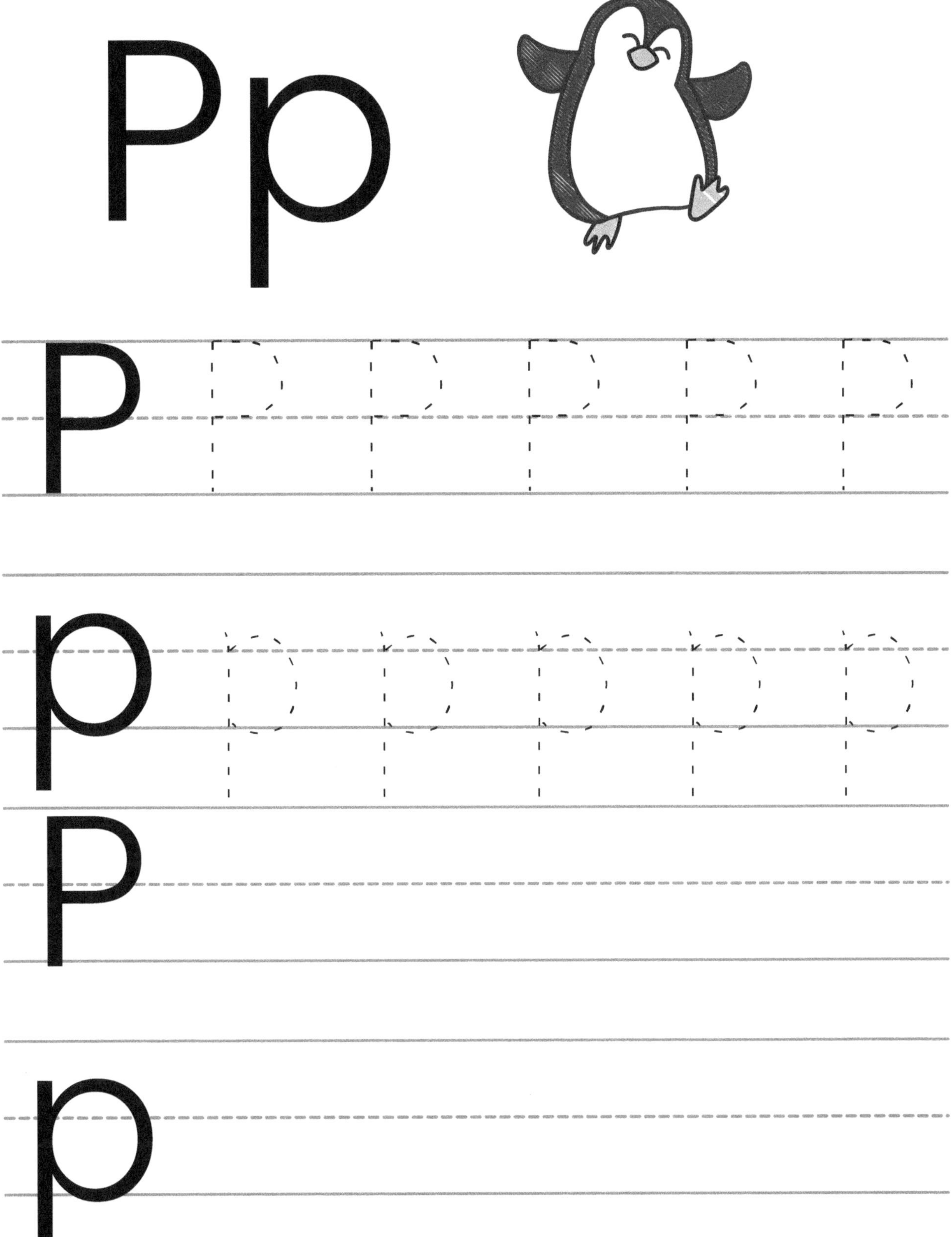

DIRECTIONS: TRACE THE WORDS THAT BEGIN WITH THE LETTER P

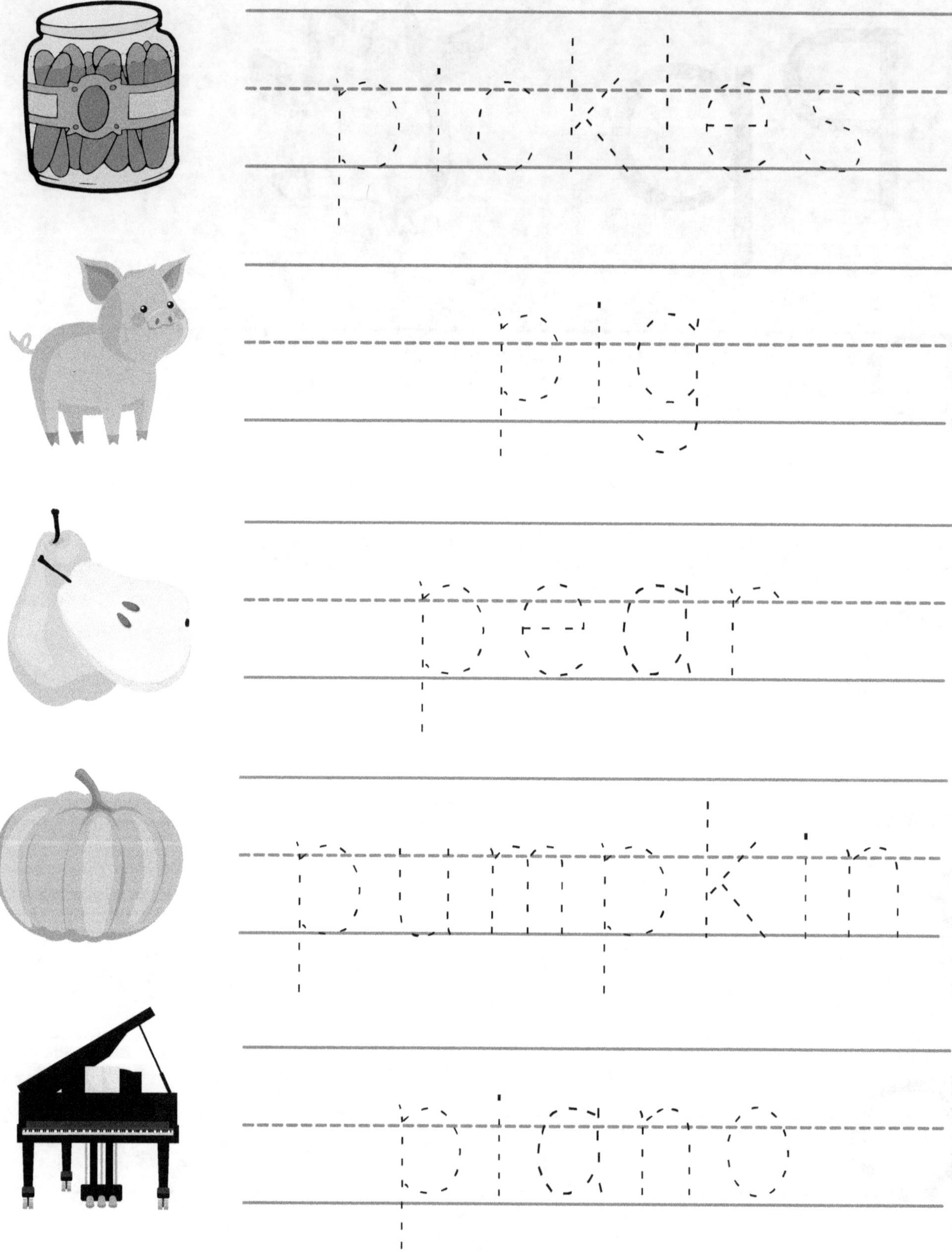

FIND THE LETTERS.

DIRECTIONS: TRACE THE LETTERS. THEN COLOR THE CIRCLES THAT HAVE THE LETTER YOU TRACED.

PP is for Pig

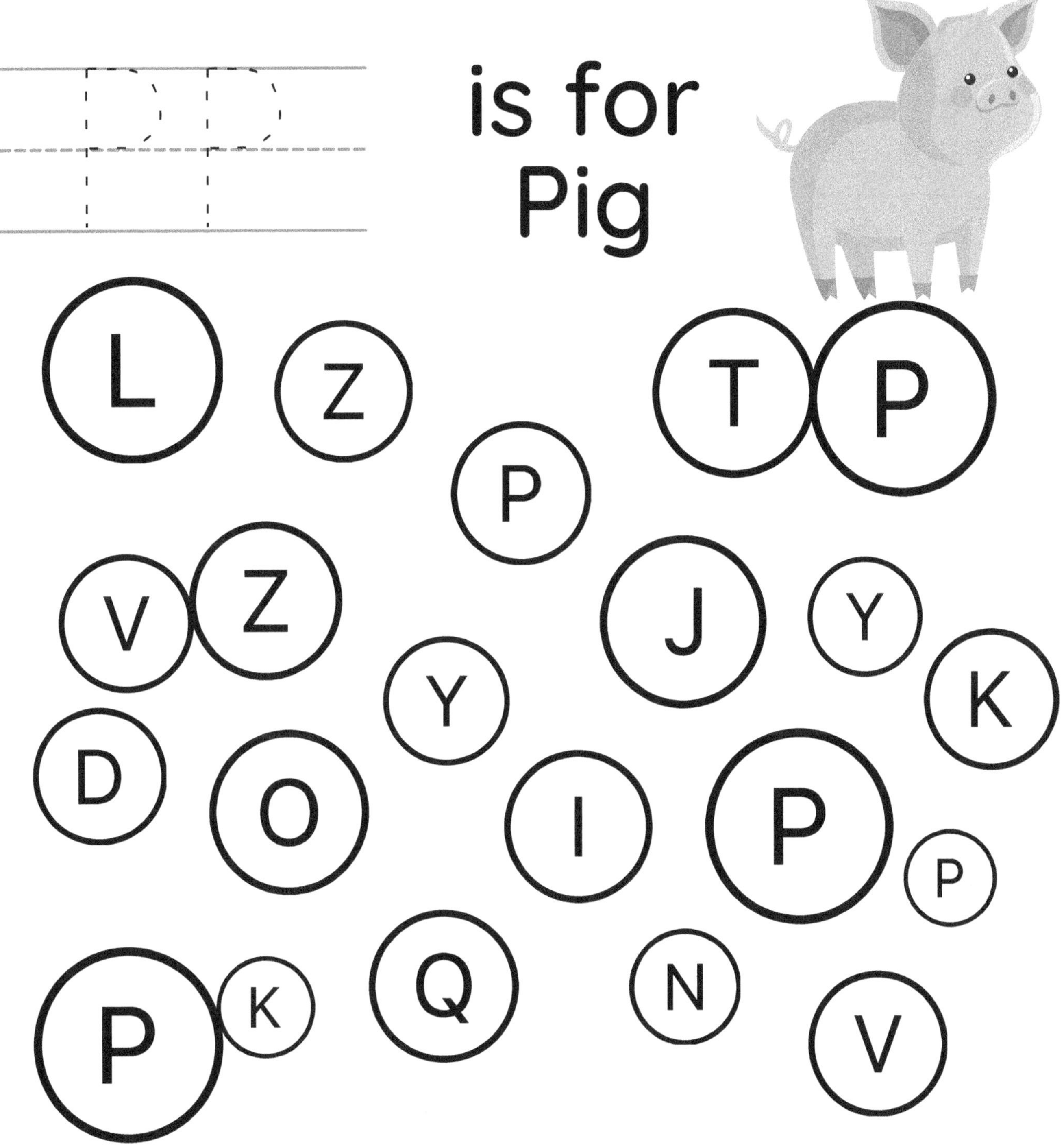

Directions: practice writting each letters in the space provided

Qq

DIRECTIONS: TRACE THE WORDS THAT BEGIN WITH THE LETTER Q

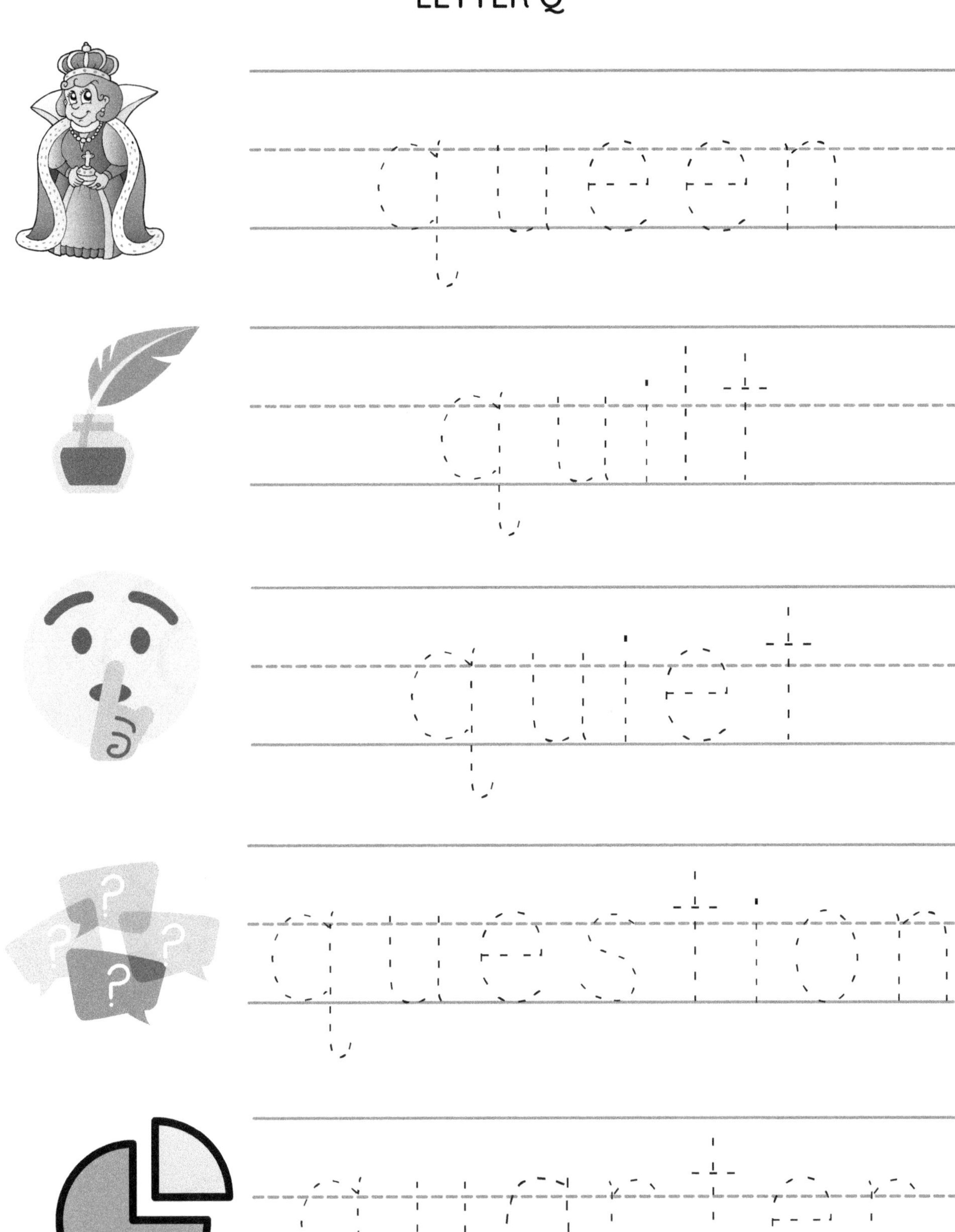

FIND THE LETTERS.

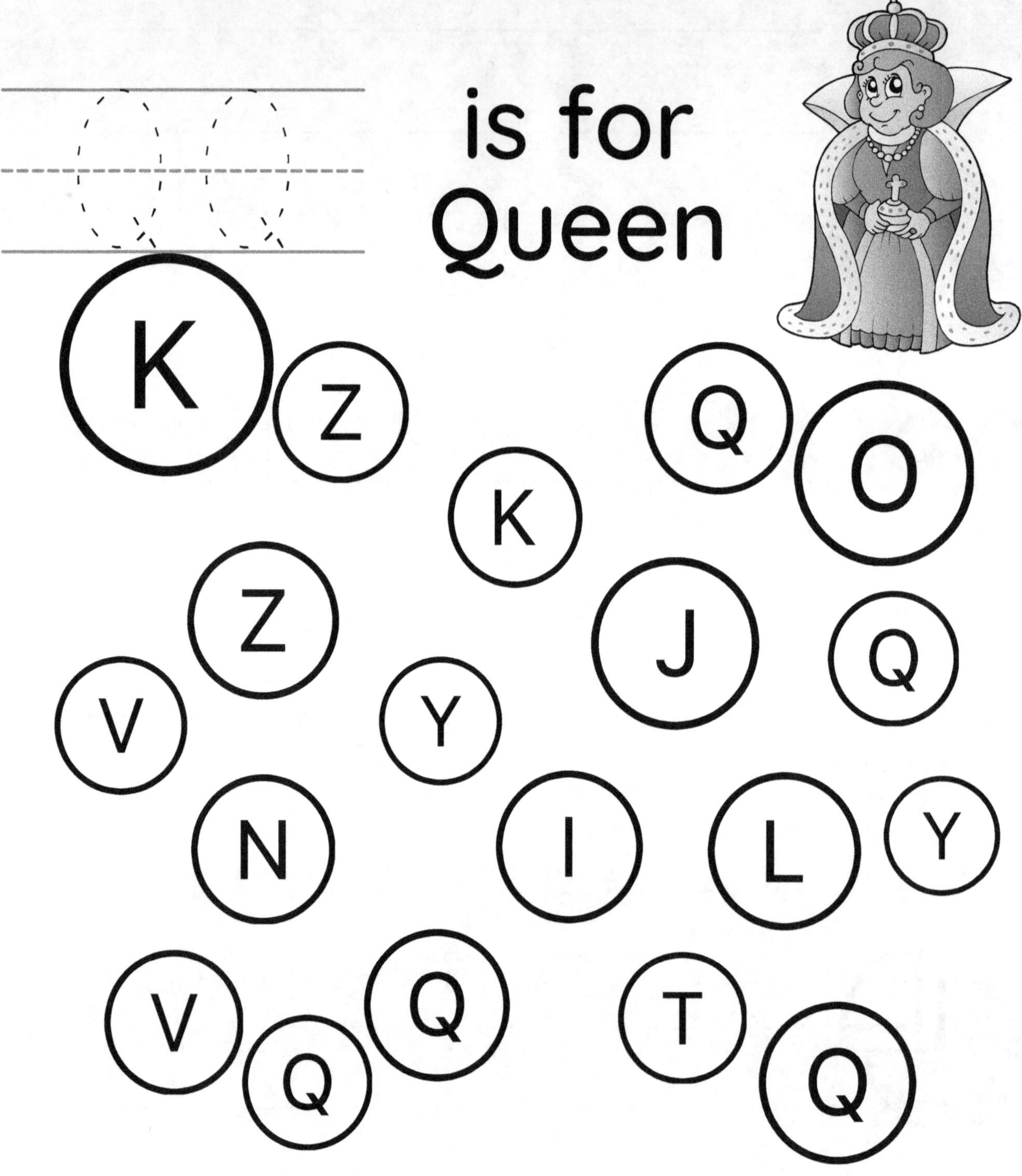

DIRECTIONS: PRACTICE WRITING EACH LETTER IN THE SPACE PROVIDED.

R r

R R R R R R R

r r r r r r

R

r

DIRECTIONS: TRACE THE WORDS THAT BEGIN WITH THE LETTER R

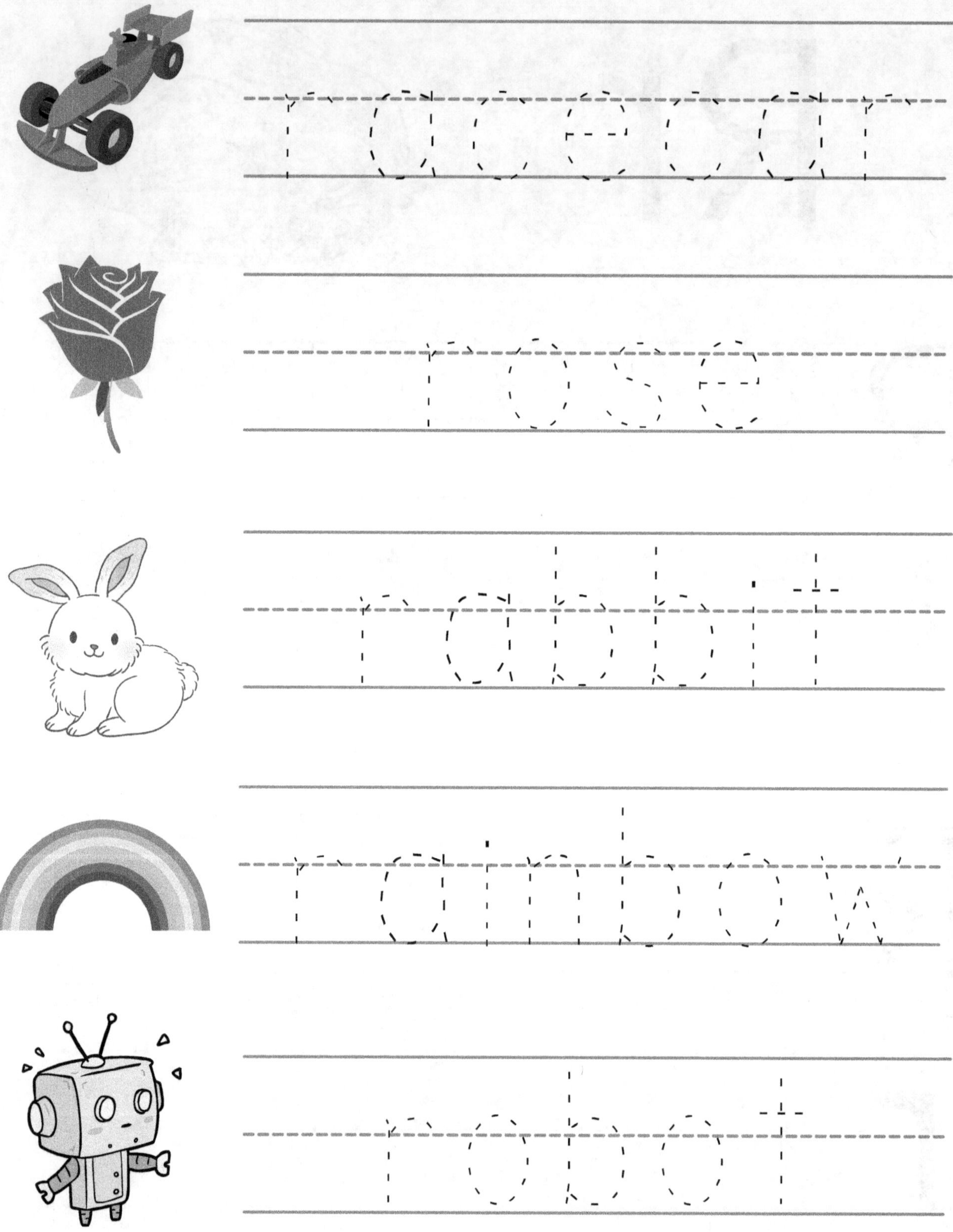

FIND THE LETTERS.

DIRECTIONS: TRACE THE LETTERS. THEN COLOR THE
CIRCLES THAT HAVE THE LETTER YOU TRACED.

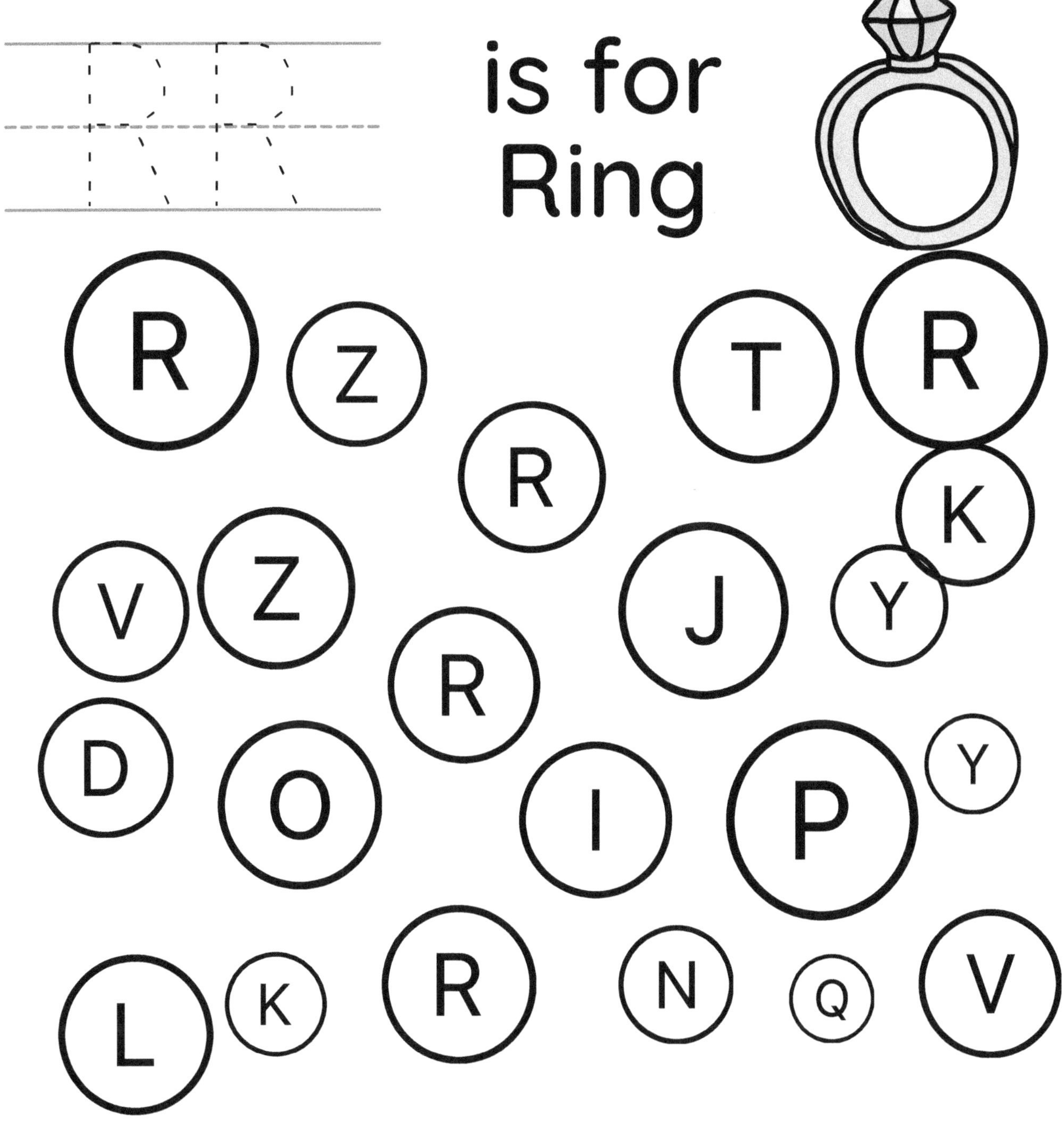

is for
Ring

S

S

S

S

DIRECTIONS: TRACE THE WORDS THAT BEGIN WITH THE LETTER S

FIND THE LETTERS.

DIRECTIONS: TRACE THE LETTERS. THEN COLOR THE
CIRCLES THAT HAVE THE LETTER YOU TRACED.

is for
Snake

DIRECTIONS: PRACTICE WRITING EACH LETTER IN THE SPACE PROVIDED.

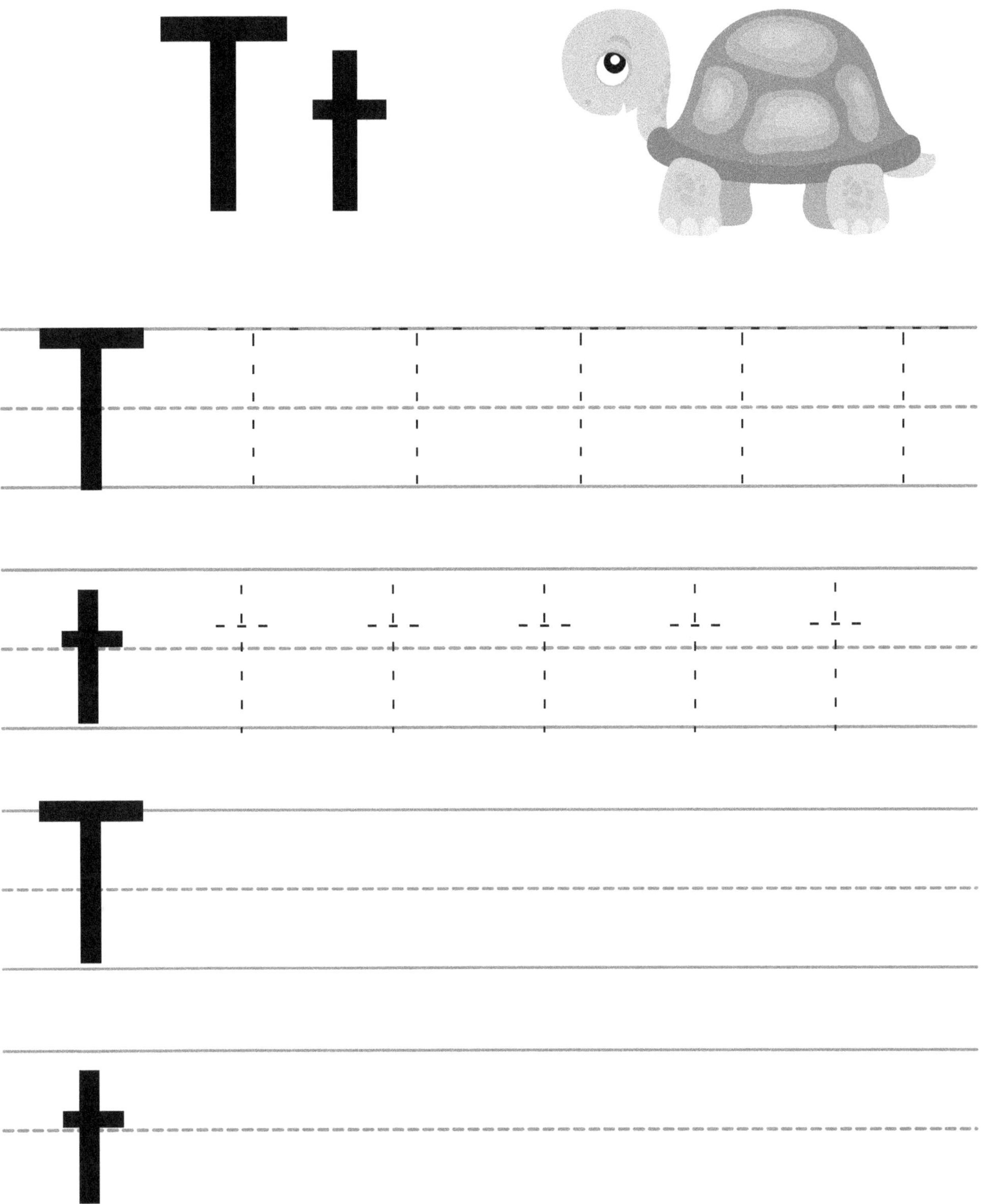

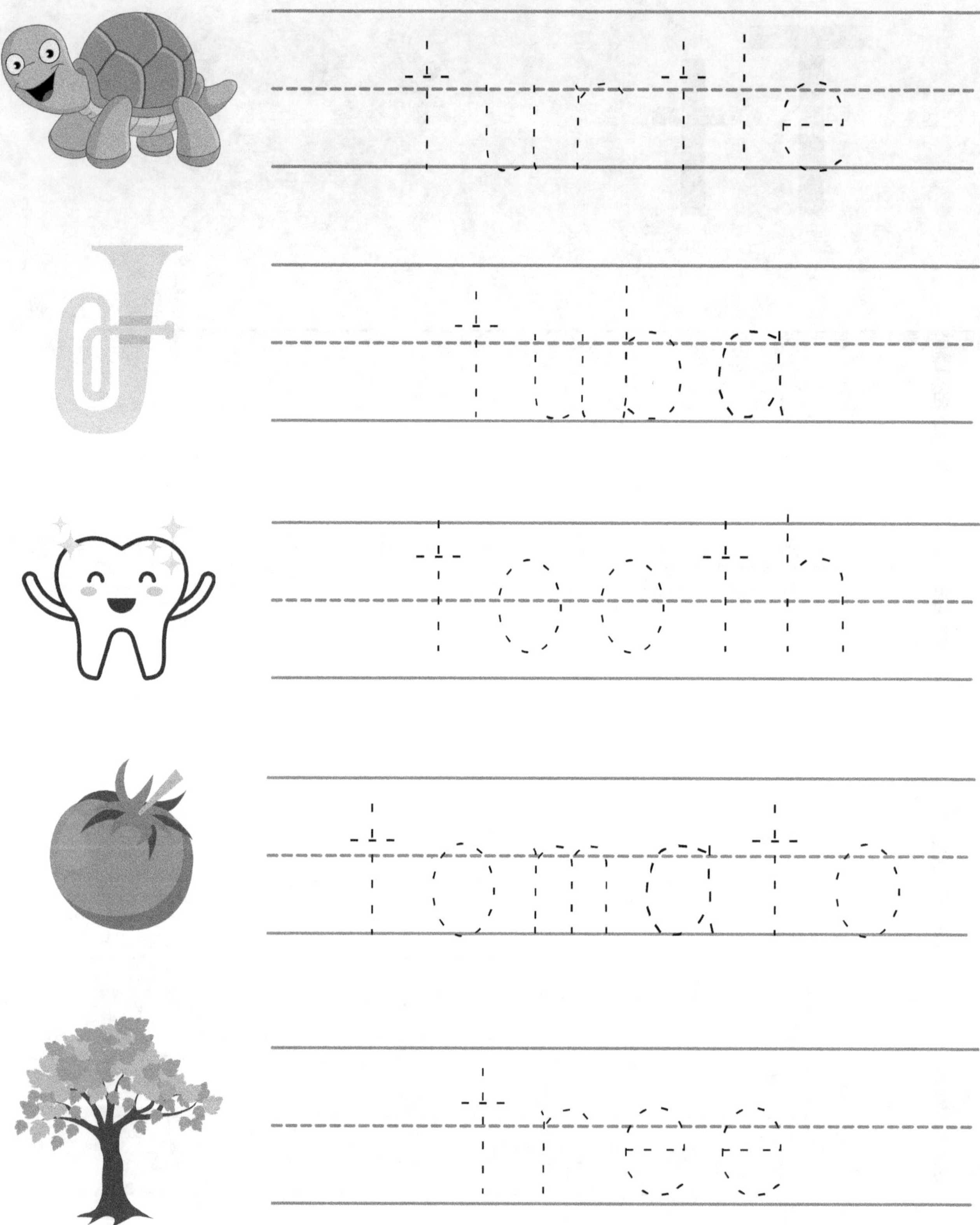

DIRECTIONS: TRACE THE WORDS THAT BEGIN WITH THE LETTER T

FIND THE LETTERS.

DIRECTIONS: TRACE THE LETTERS. THEN COLOR THE
CIRCLES THAT HAVE THE LETTER YOU TRACED.

is for
Tiger

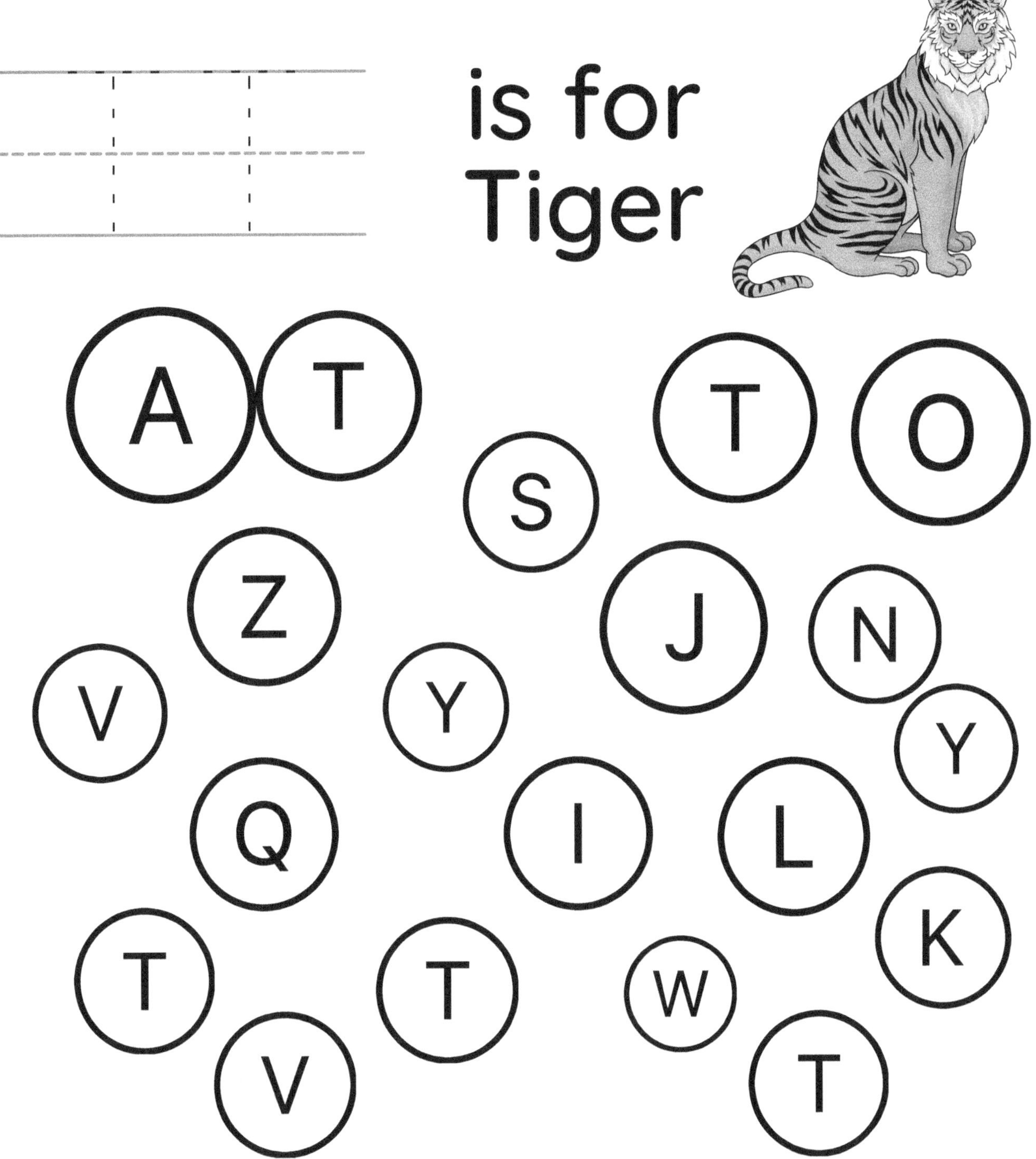

DIRECTIONS: PRACTICE WRITING EACH LETTER IN THE SPACE PROVIDED.

FIND THE LETTERS.

DIRECTIONS: TRACE THE LETTERS. THEN COLOR THE
CIRCLES THAT HAVE THE LETTER YOU TRACED.

is for
UFO

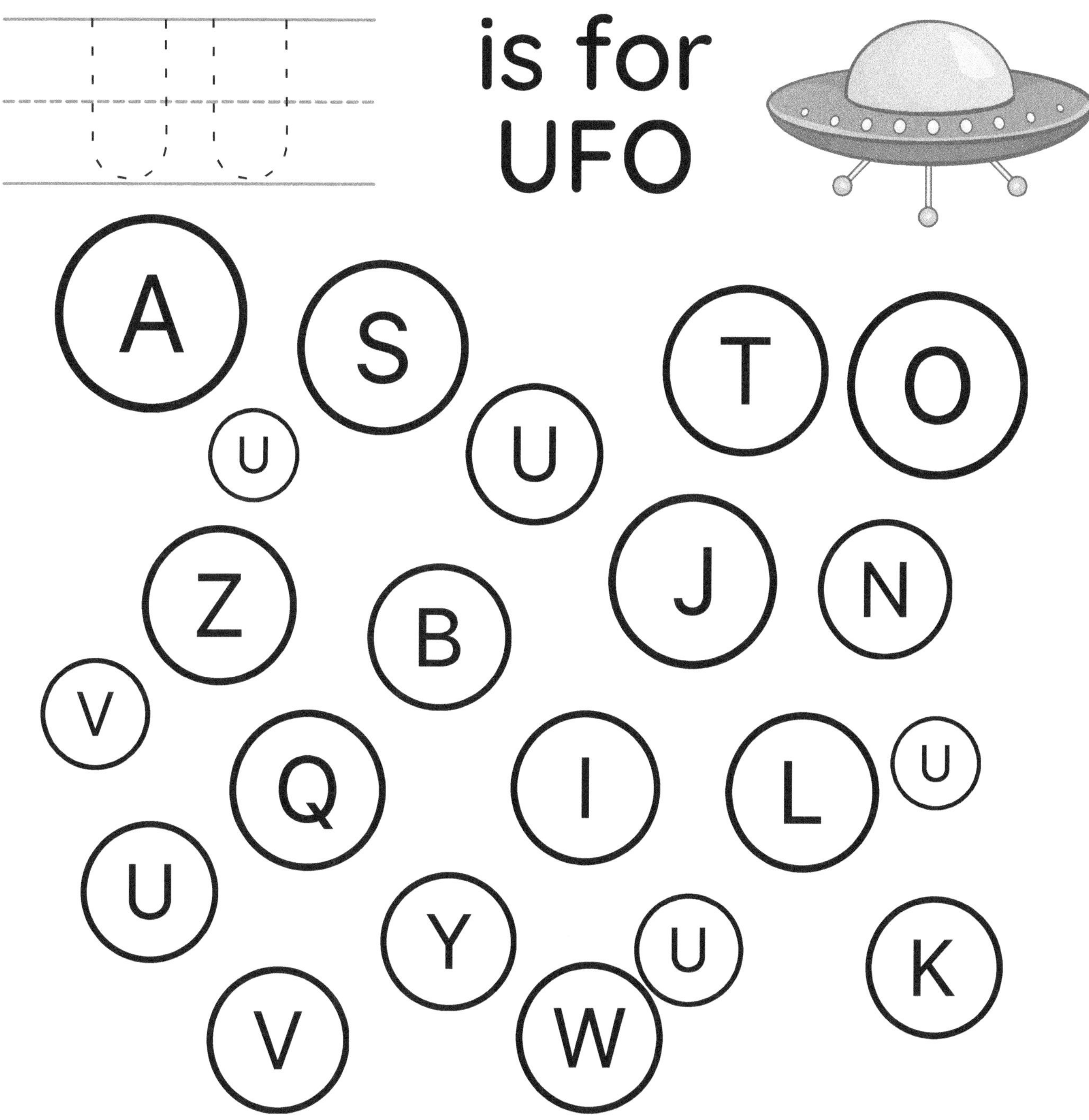

DIRECTIONS: PRACTICE WRITING EACH LETTER IN THE SPACE PROVIDED.

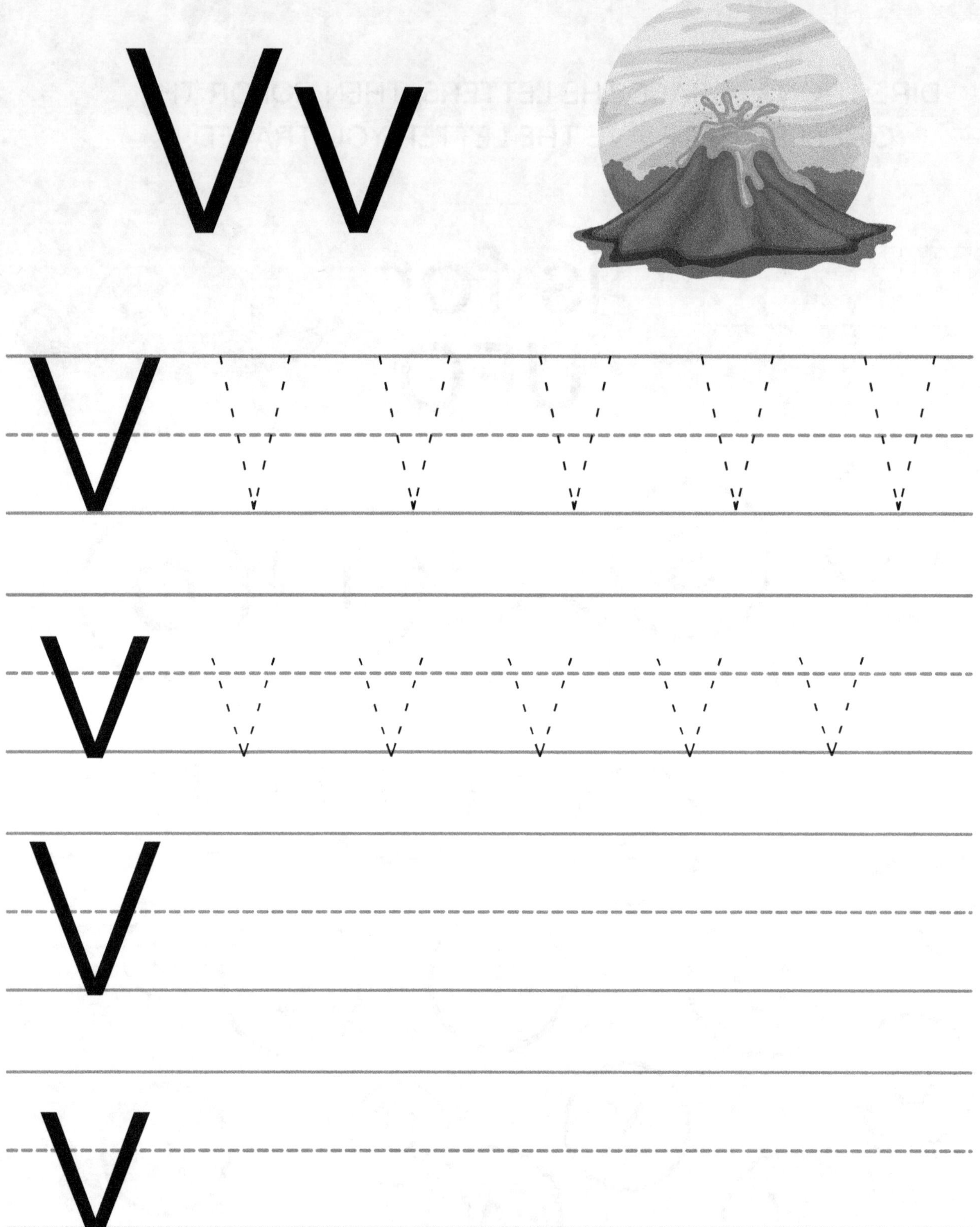

DIRECTIONS: TRACE THE WORDS THAT BEGIN WITH THE LETTER V

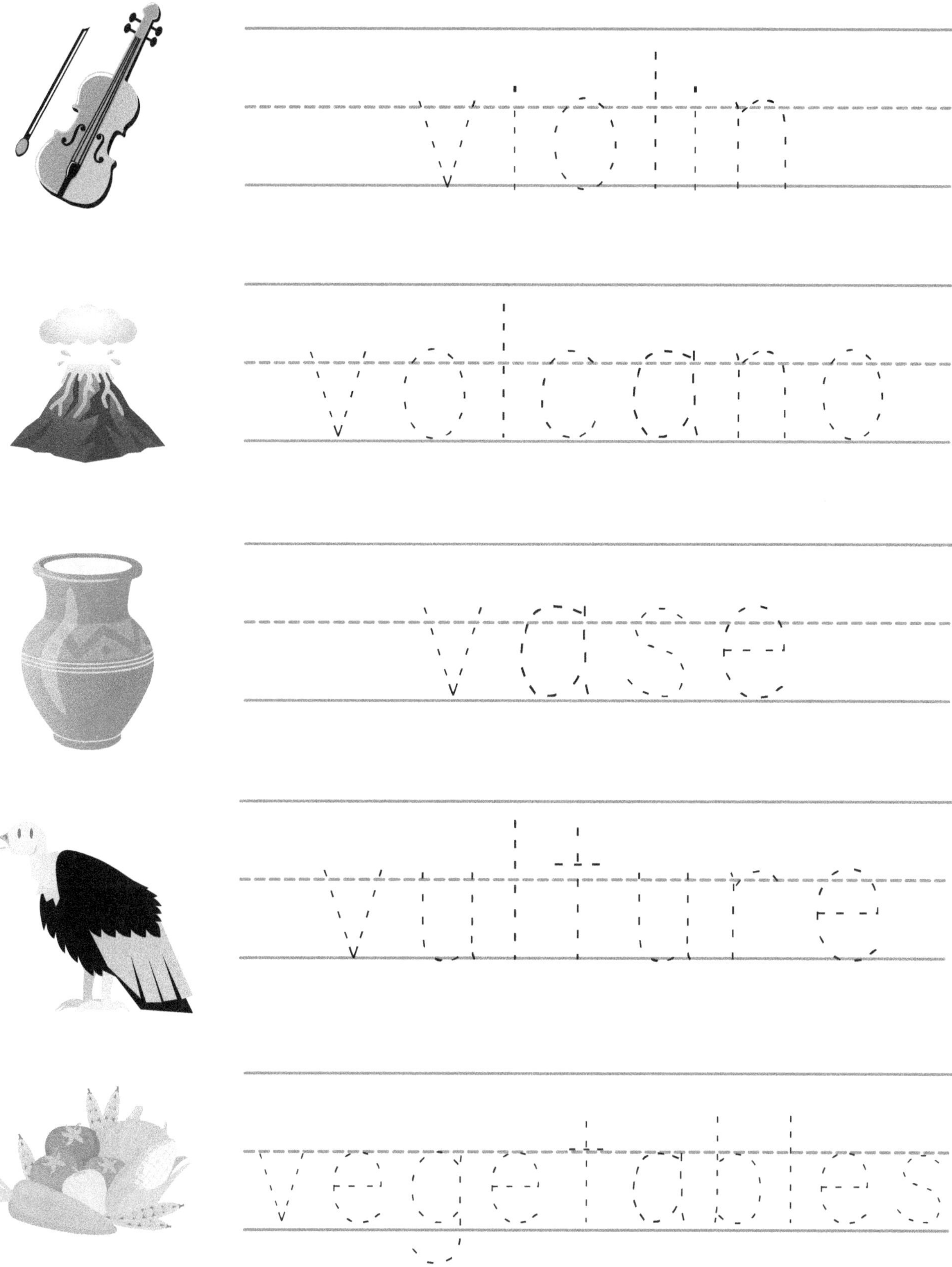

FIND THE LETTERS.

DIRECTIONS: TRACE THE LETTERS. THEN COLOR THE
CIRCLES THAT HAVE THE LETTER YOU TRACED.

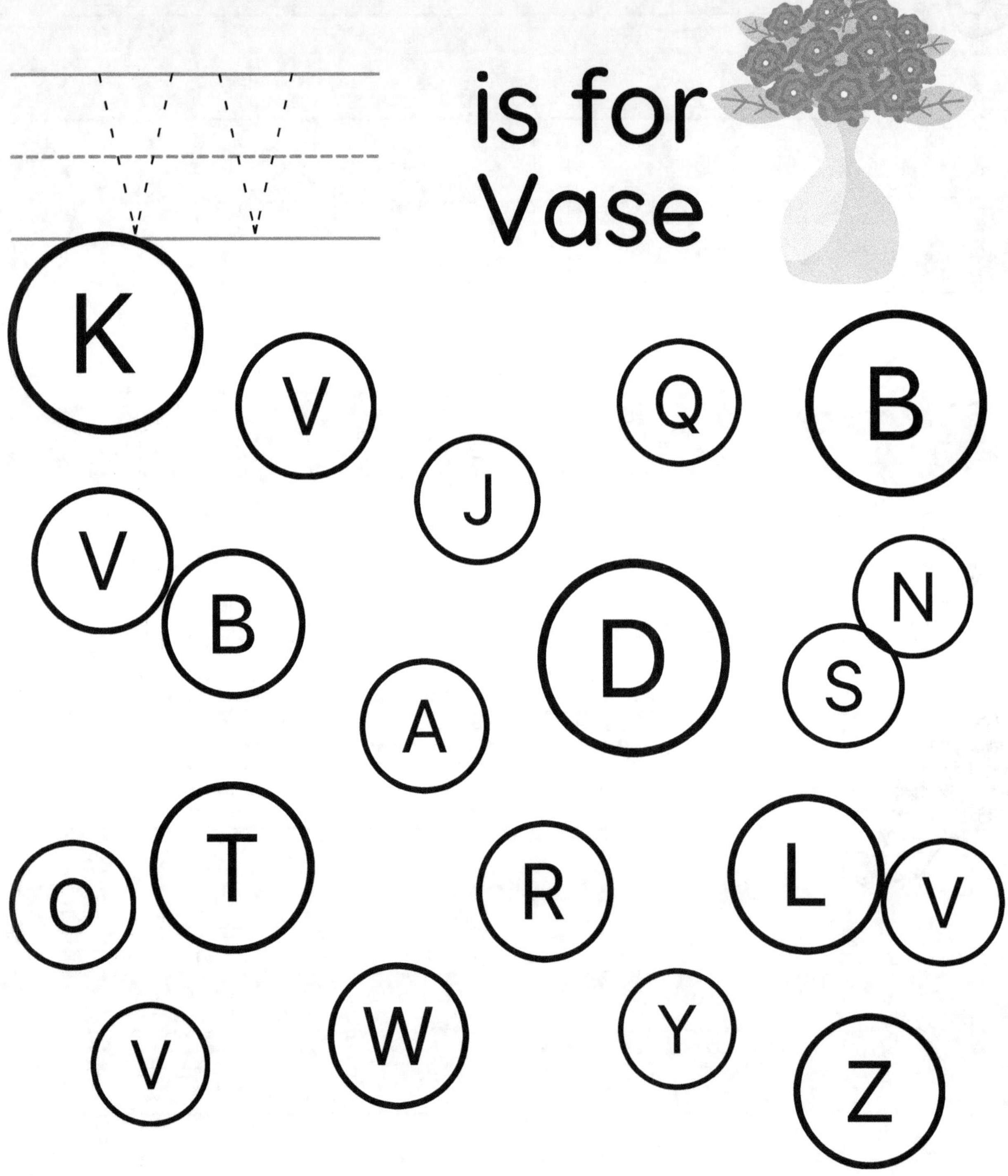

DIRECTIONS: PRACTICE WRITING EACH LETTER IN THE SPACE PROVIDED.

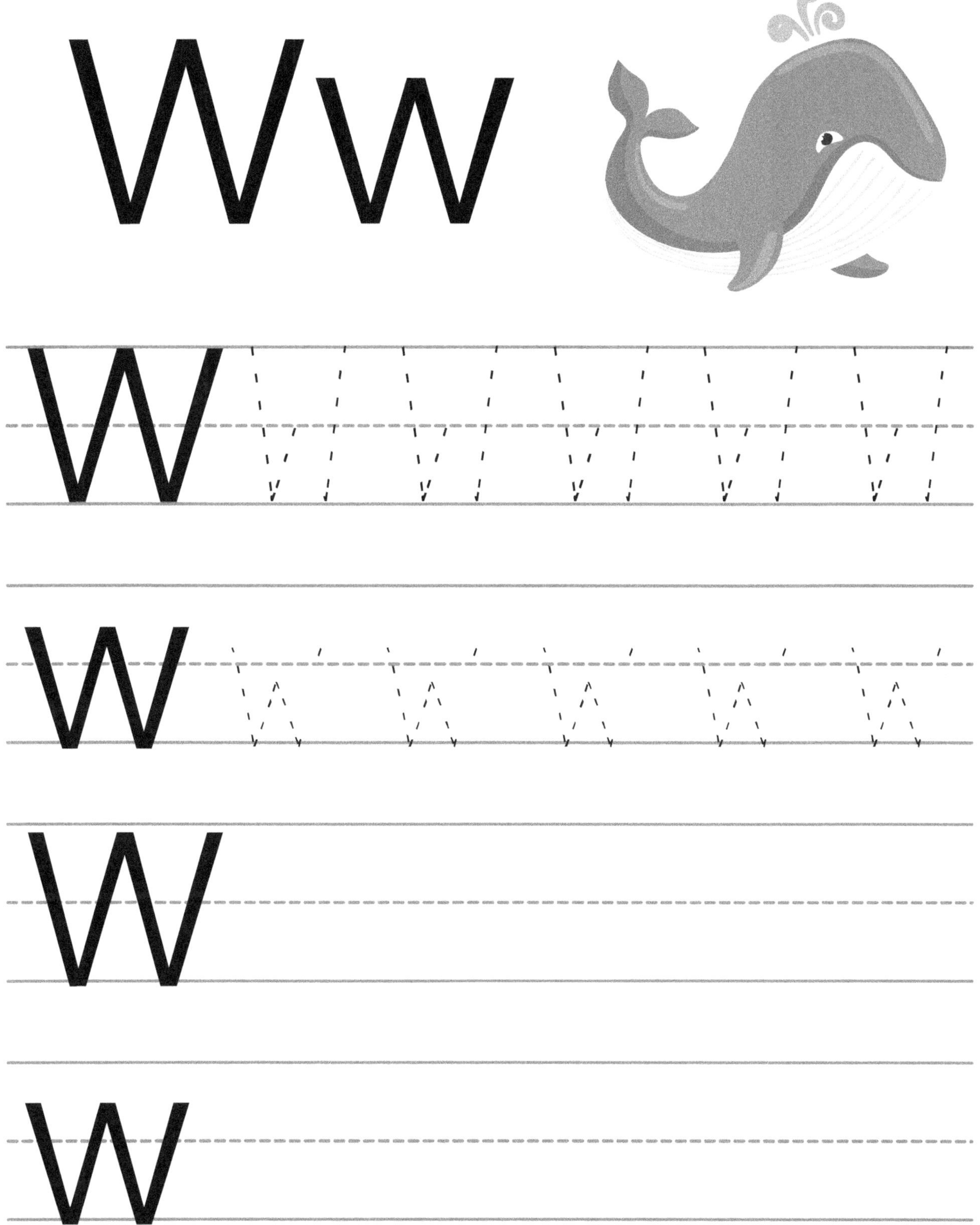

DIRECTIONS: TRACE THE WORDS THAT BEGIN WITH THE
LETTER W

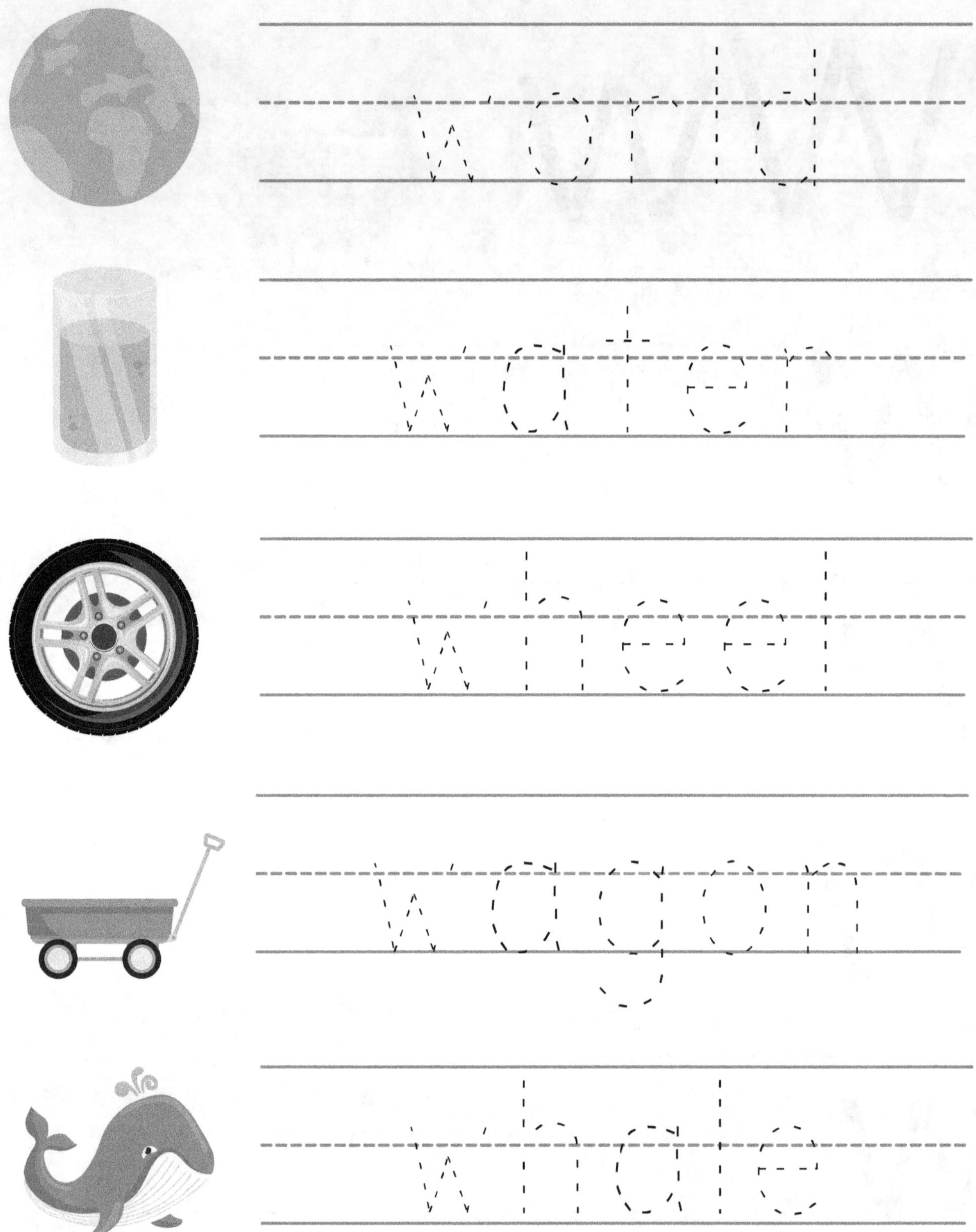

world
water
wheel
wagon
whale

FIND THE LETTERS.

DIRECTIONS: TRACE THE LETTERS. THEN COLOR THE
CIRCLES THAT HAVE THE LETTER YOU TRACED.

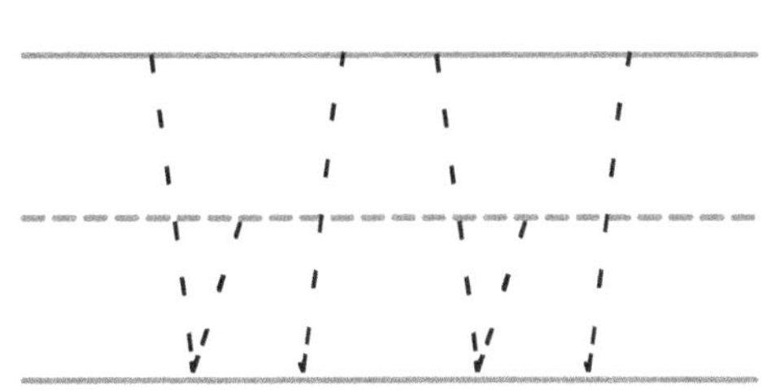

is for **Whale**

S Z T O
W
Z J W
Y K
V Q I L K
W N
W W
V

DIRECTIONS: PRACTICE WRITING EACH LETTER IN THE SPACE PROVIDED.

Xx

X X X X X X

x x x x x x

X

x

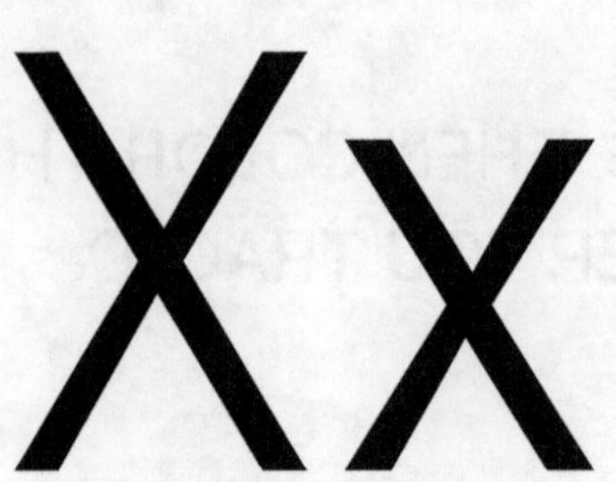

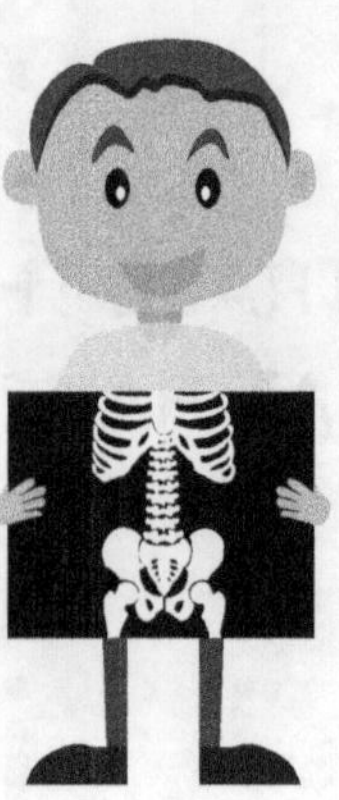

FIND THE LETTERS.

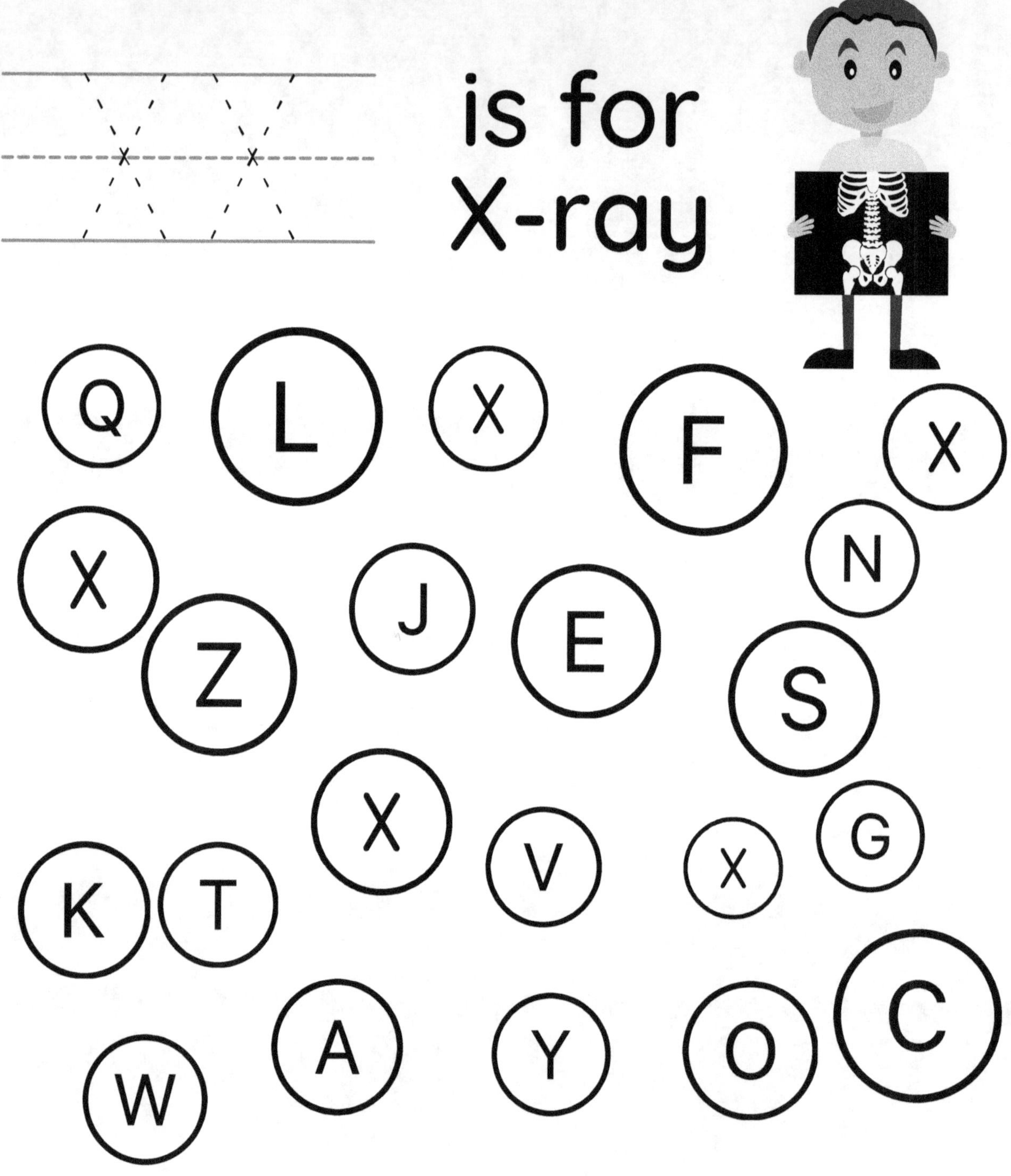

DIRECTIONS: PRACTICE WRITING EACH LETTER IN THE SPACE PROVIDED.

DIRECTIONS: TRACE THE WORDS THAT BEGIN WITH THE LETTER Y

FIND THE LETTERS.

DIRECTIONS: TRACE THE LETTERS. THEN COLOR THE
CIRCLES THAT HAVE THE LETTER YOU TRACED.

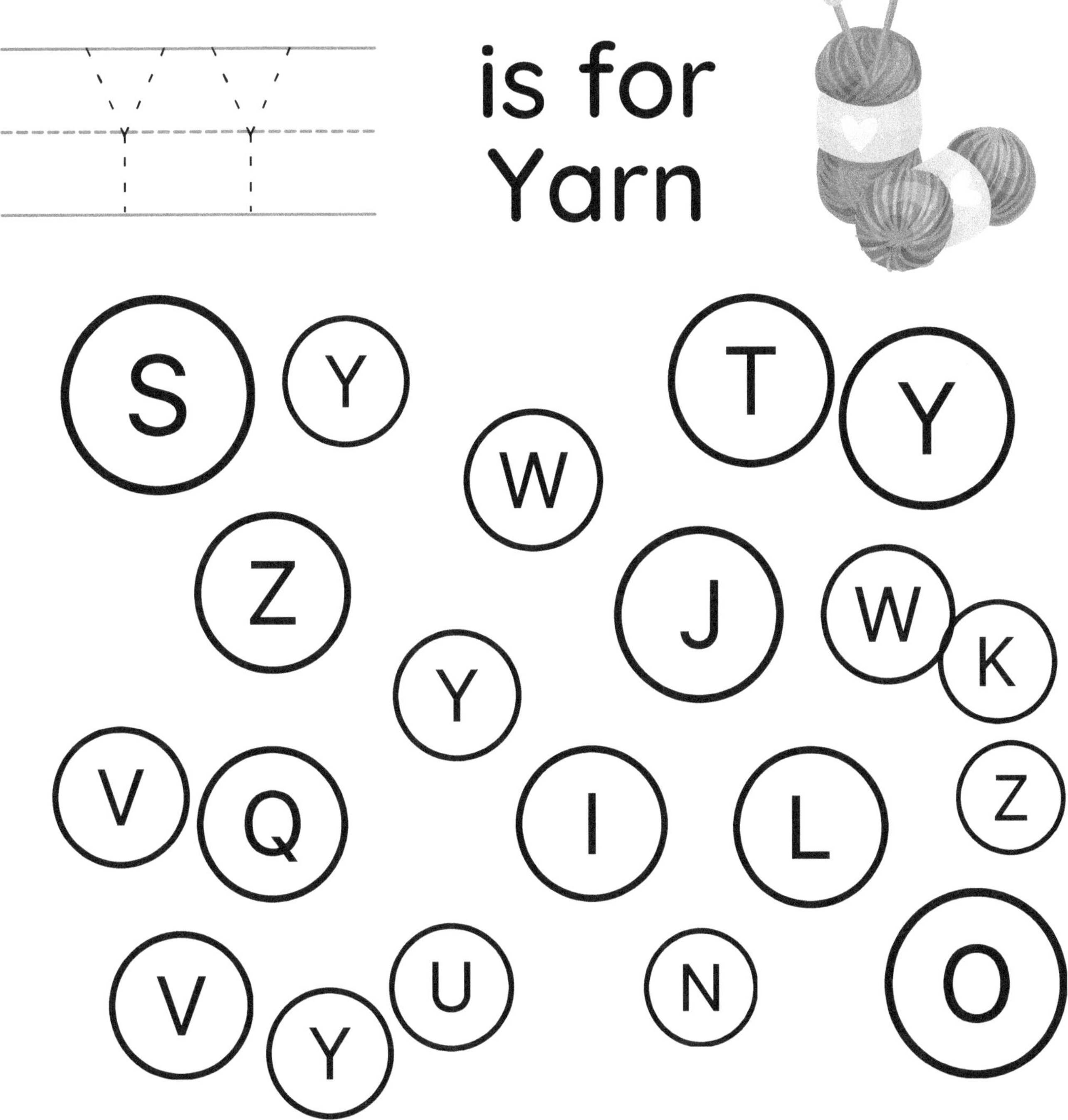

is for
Yarn

S   Y   T   Y
W
Z   J   W   K
Y
V   Q   I   L   Z
V   Y   U   N   O

DIRECTIONS: PRACTICE WRITING EACH LETTER IN THE SPACE PROVIDED.

Zz

DIRECTIONS: TRACE THE WORDS THAT BEGIN WITH THE LETTER Z

FIND THE LETTERS.

DIRECTIONS: TRACE THE LETTERS. THEN COLOR THE
CIRCLES THAT HAVE THE LETTER YOU TRACED.

is for
Zebra

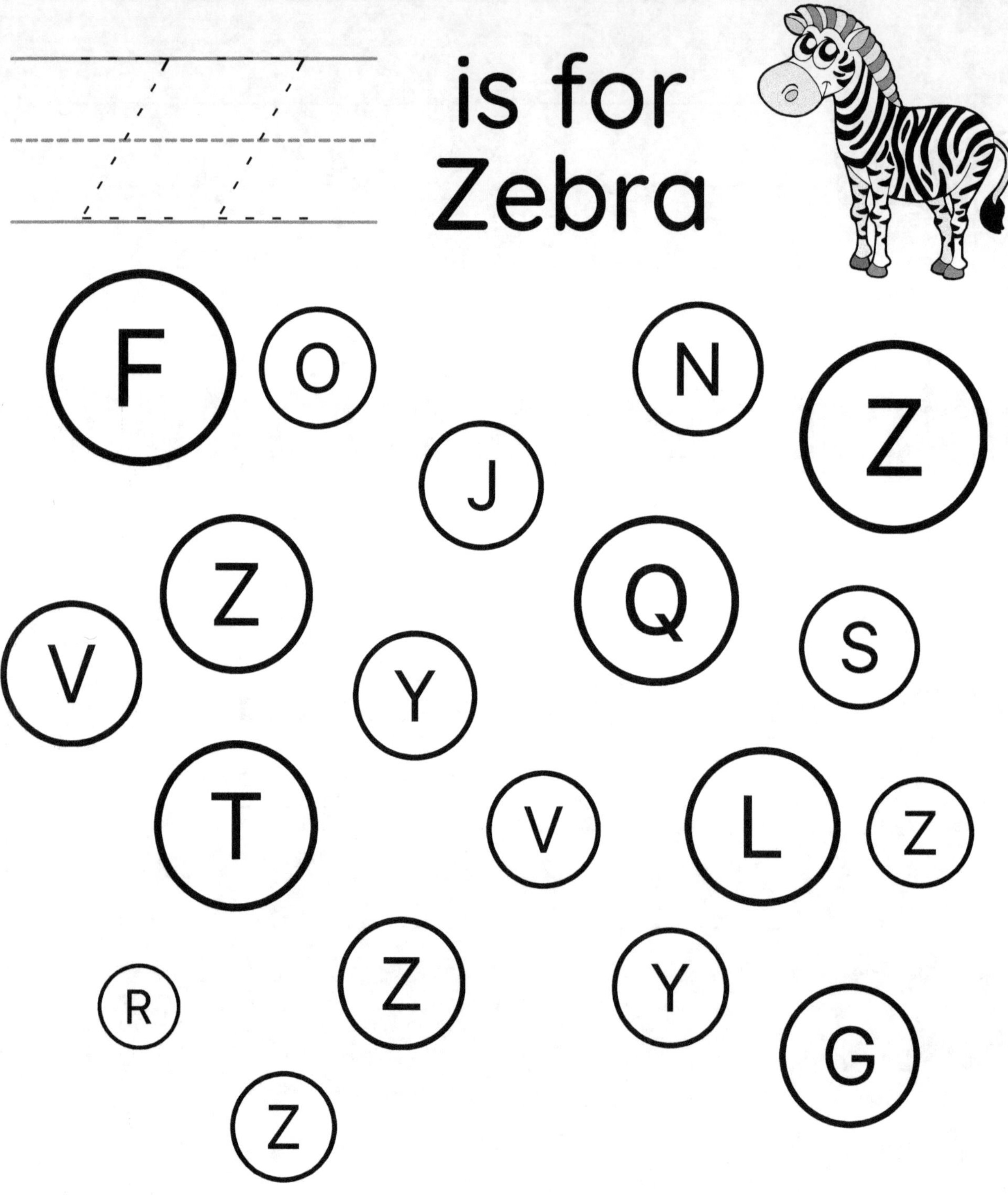